The PUMPKIN SPICE CAFÉ
COLORING BOOK

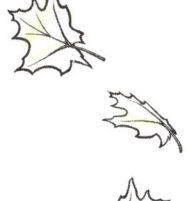

Illustrated by Nicolette Cavern

Laurie Gilmore is a No. 1 *Sunday Times* bestseller and a *USA Today* bestseller who writes steamy small-town romance. Her Dream Harbor series is filled with quirky townsfolk, cozy settings and swoon-worthy romance. *The Pumpkin Spice Café* was featured on *Good Morning America*, and was named the TikTok Shop Book of the Year 2024.

She loves finding books with the perfect balance of sweetness and spice and strives for that in her own writing.

The DREAM HARBOR SERIES

The PUMPKIN SPICE CAFÉ
The CINNAMON BUN BOOK STORE
The CHRISTMAS TREE FARM
The STRAWBERRY PATCH PANCAKE HOUSE
The GINGERBREAD BAKERY

"Let's go grab a drink before you turn into a pumpkin"

"Everything was better
in Dream Harbor"

"The orchard was open for pick-your-own apples and pumpkins, with a hayride pulled by his grandfather atop his trusty tractor"

"Jeanie glanced down at the cat that had taken up residence on her stomach. She supposed he had some calming qualities, like the gentle vibration currently emanating from him now"

"The wind was crisp and cold, shaking the colorful leaves from the trees. The sun had set hours ago, making it feel later than it was"

"Hot-cider-and-pumpkin-spiced everything goes great with my seasonal muffins and pies"

"They all sat at a round high-top table, mugs and plates of leftover goodies from the bakery laid out between them. It was another day of rain and the café was dim but cozy, the windows fogged up with the warmth from inside. Someone had drawn a heart in the condensation earlier in the day and it was still there, a happy little doodle standing out in the gloom"

"Jeanie's real smile was even more endearing than the damn hedgehogs"

"Little pumpkins were on every table and counter, providing just the right amount of fall-y-ness"

"Annie was selling pies and cookies, and anything made with apples or pumpkins, or cinnamon-spiced"

"Happy Fall Festival!"

"A laidback, quaint, small-town life"

"There were three kinds of potato chips, corn chips, and guac; pretzels in several shapes, a jumbo-sized bag of mini candy bars intended for trick-or-treaters; Twizzlers (which Jeanie hated, but thought Logan might like), fresh-baked cookies from Annie's bakery; and she had a pizza on the way"

"She made herself comfortable at his little table. Outside the weather was gray and cold. Logan wouldn't be surprised if there was a layer of wet snow on the ground tomorrow morning. But today it was warm and cozy inside his little apartment"

"This man was the picture of autumnal bounty with his crate of vegetables and his worn, flannel shirt and thick beard"

"The café was flanked by Annie's bakery and Mac's pub. The book store sat on the other side of the bakery. Add in a few other shops and restaurants, the pet store, and the post office, and that was Main Street. It was, frankly, adorable. Autumnal, small-town New England at its best"

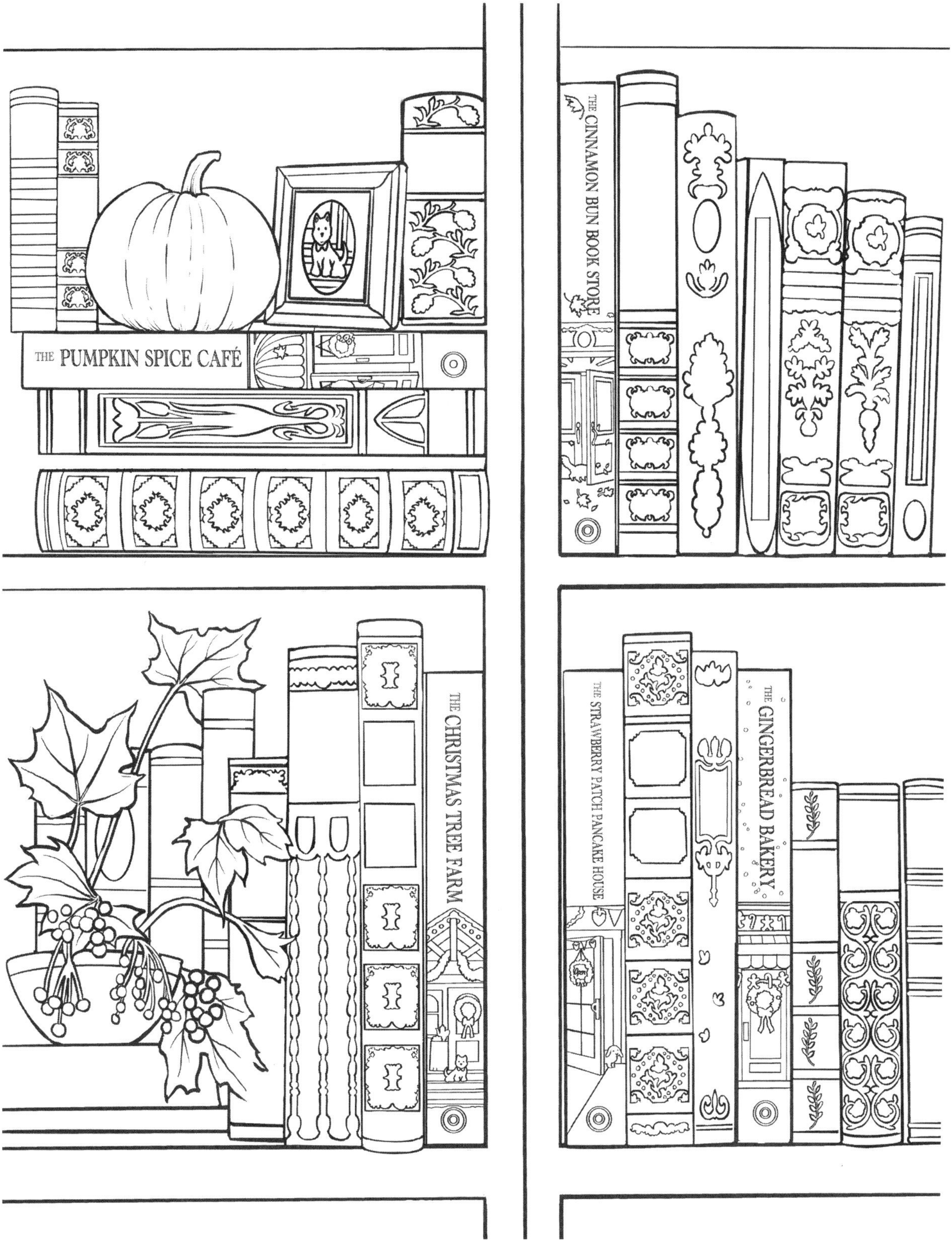
THE PUMPKIN SPICE CAFÉ
THE CINNAMON BUN BOOK STORE
THE CHRISTMAS TREE FARM
THE STRAWBERRY PATCH PANCAKE HOUSE
THE GINGERBREAD BAKERY

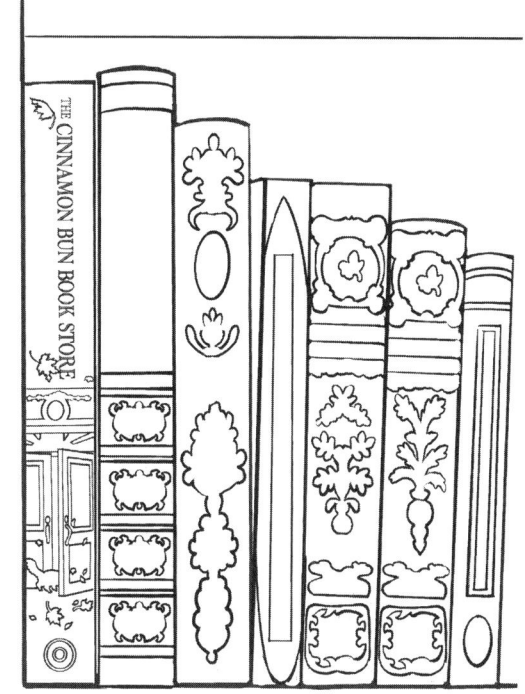

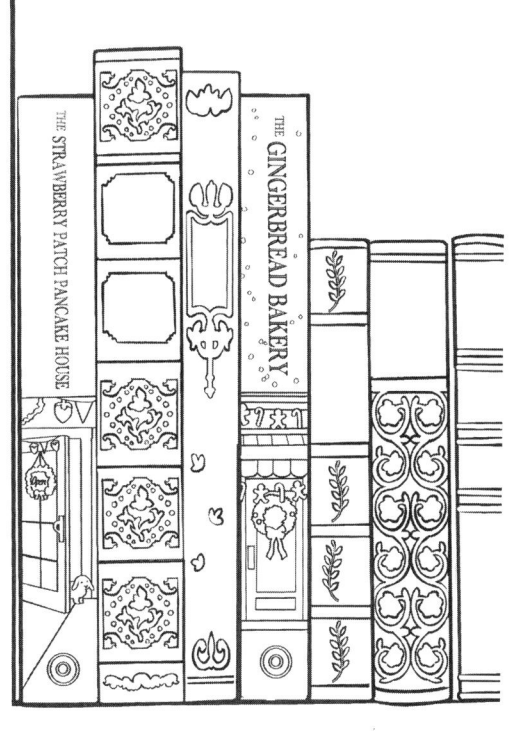

"Maybe the picture-perfect small-town life she had imagined didn't exist, but the one she had found was pretty damn perfect for her"

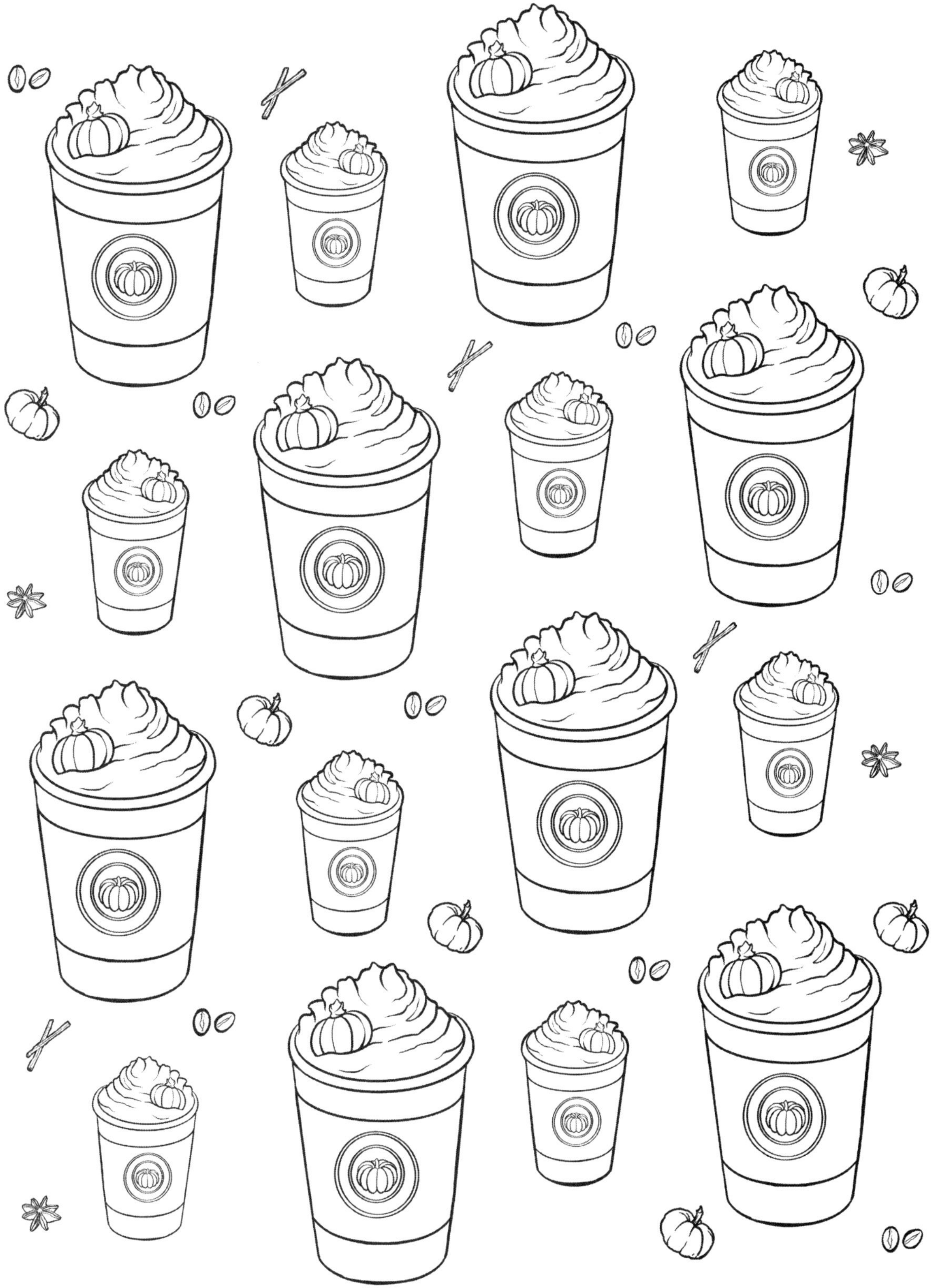

"He had to get the pumpkins there early so the festival crew could set up the pumpkin-painting table before the crowds started arriving. People spent the full day at the festival, filling up on apple-cider donuts and Annie's hand pies for breakfast, and staying straight through until dark when they lit the square with hundreds of twinkle lights and a bonfire in the park"

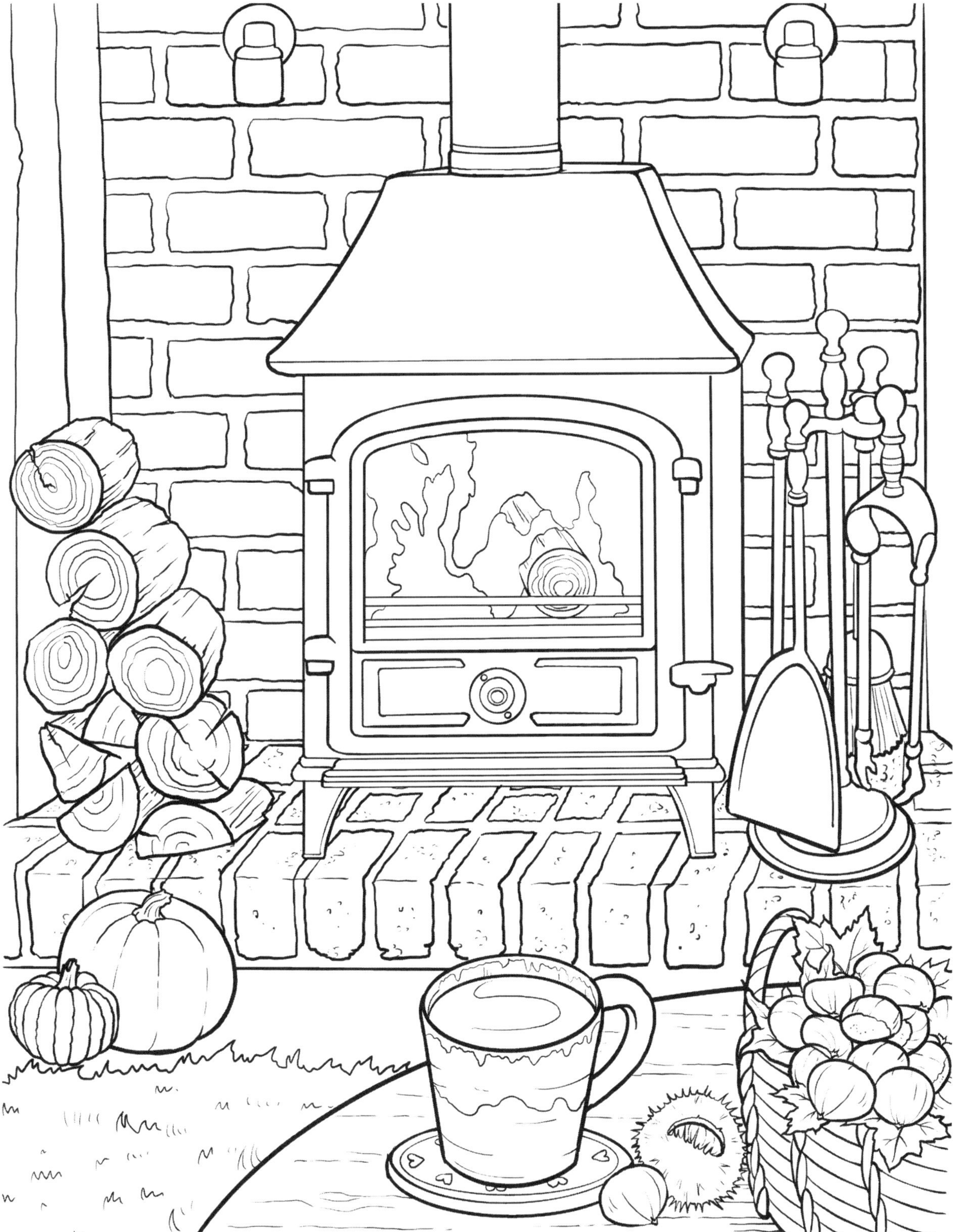

"I've loved you since I saw how many tiny pumpkins you could carry at once"

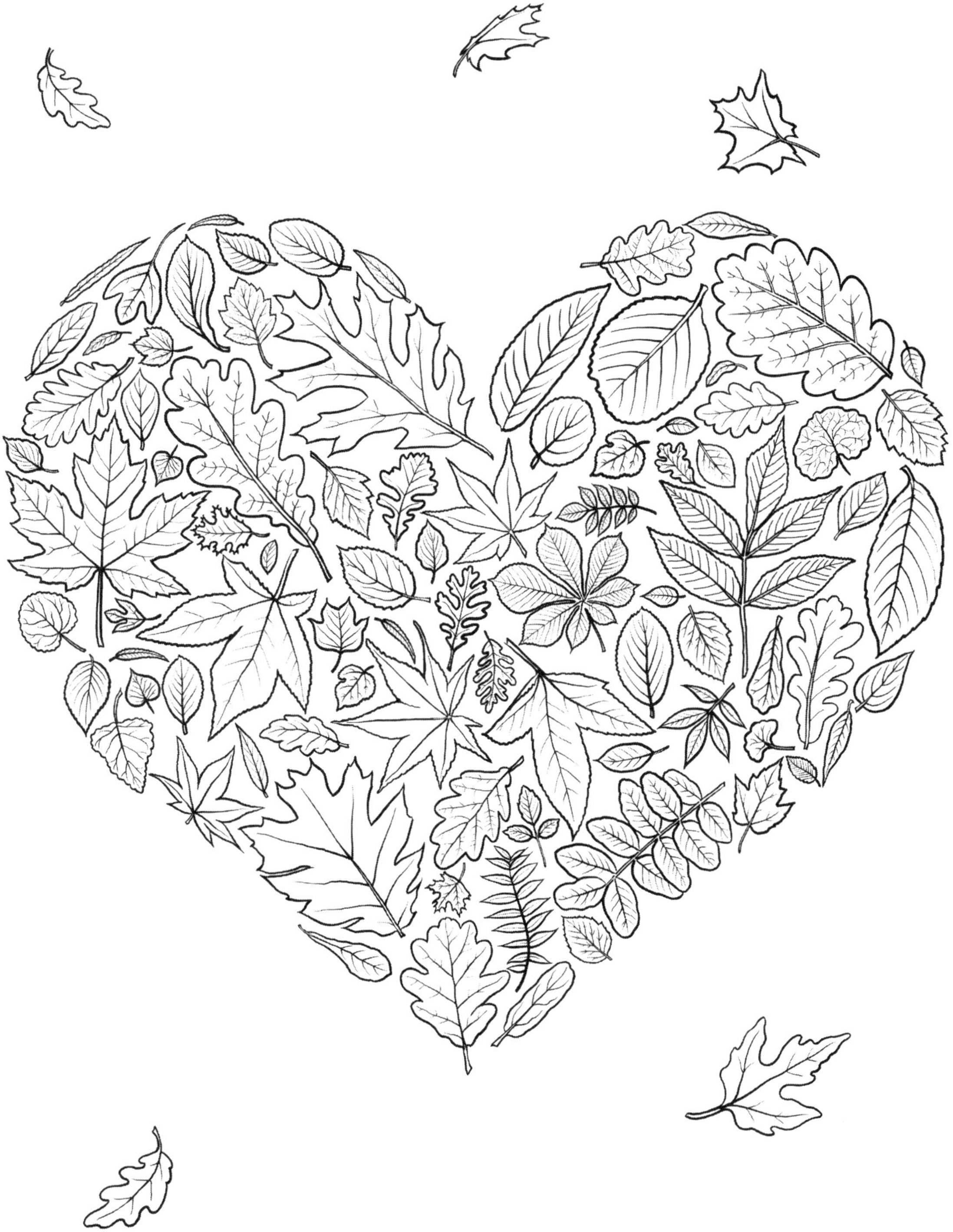

"There were tents selling all types of witchy wares: crystals and spell books and very authentic-looking witch brooms. Kids were lined up to get their faces painted, or for balloon animals, or to jump in the enormous bounce house set up on the lawn. It was madness. Delightful, apple-pie scented madness"

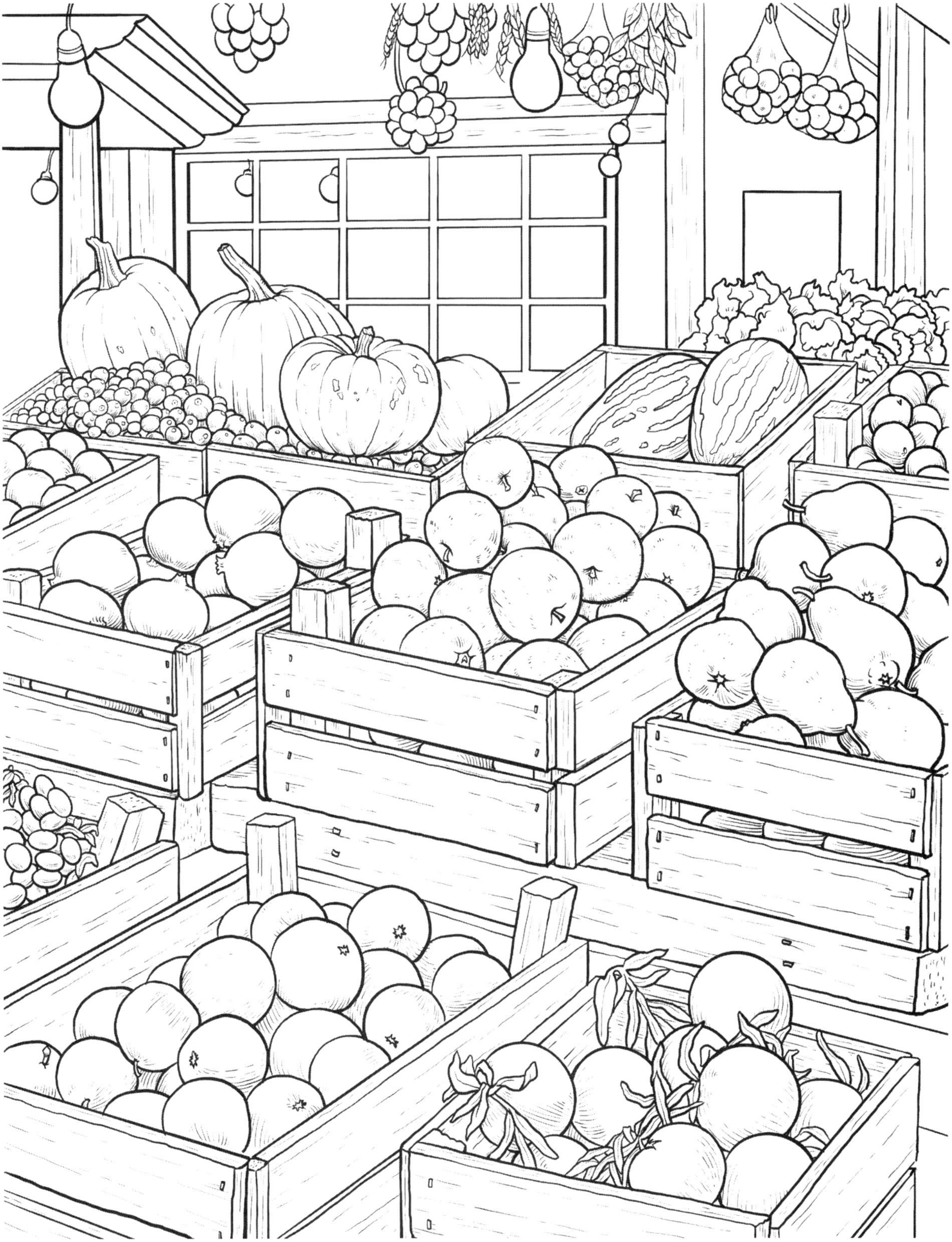

"It was still early, the sun barely over the horizon, casting the row of quaint shops in a golden glow"

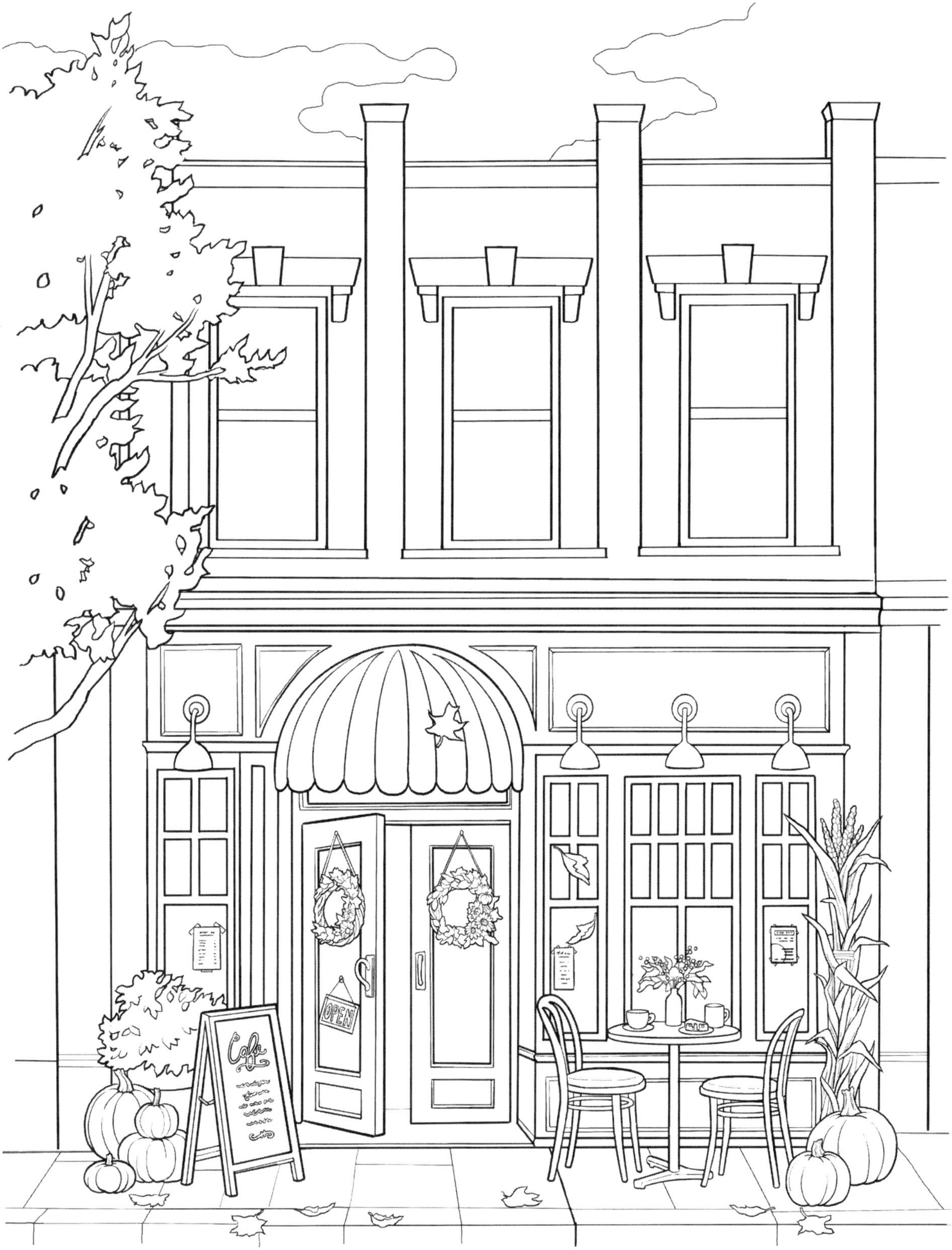
OPEN
Cafe

"She now had two chickens in her lap, and she was pretty sure one had climbed the steps and was looking for a way to perch on her head"

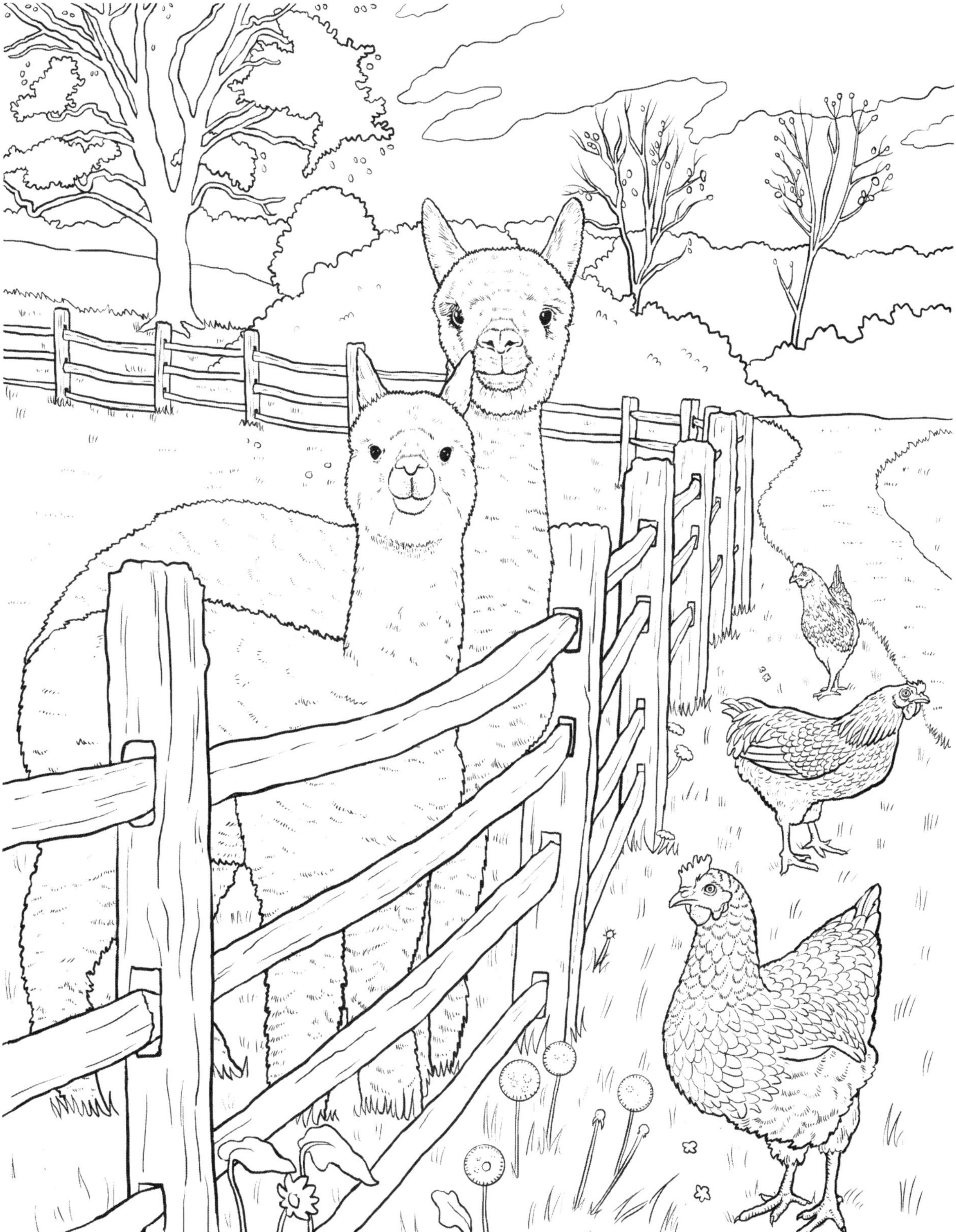

"She happily slurped her noodles, her legs tucked up under her. The rain ran in streams down the window"

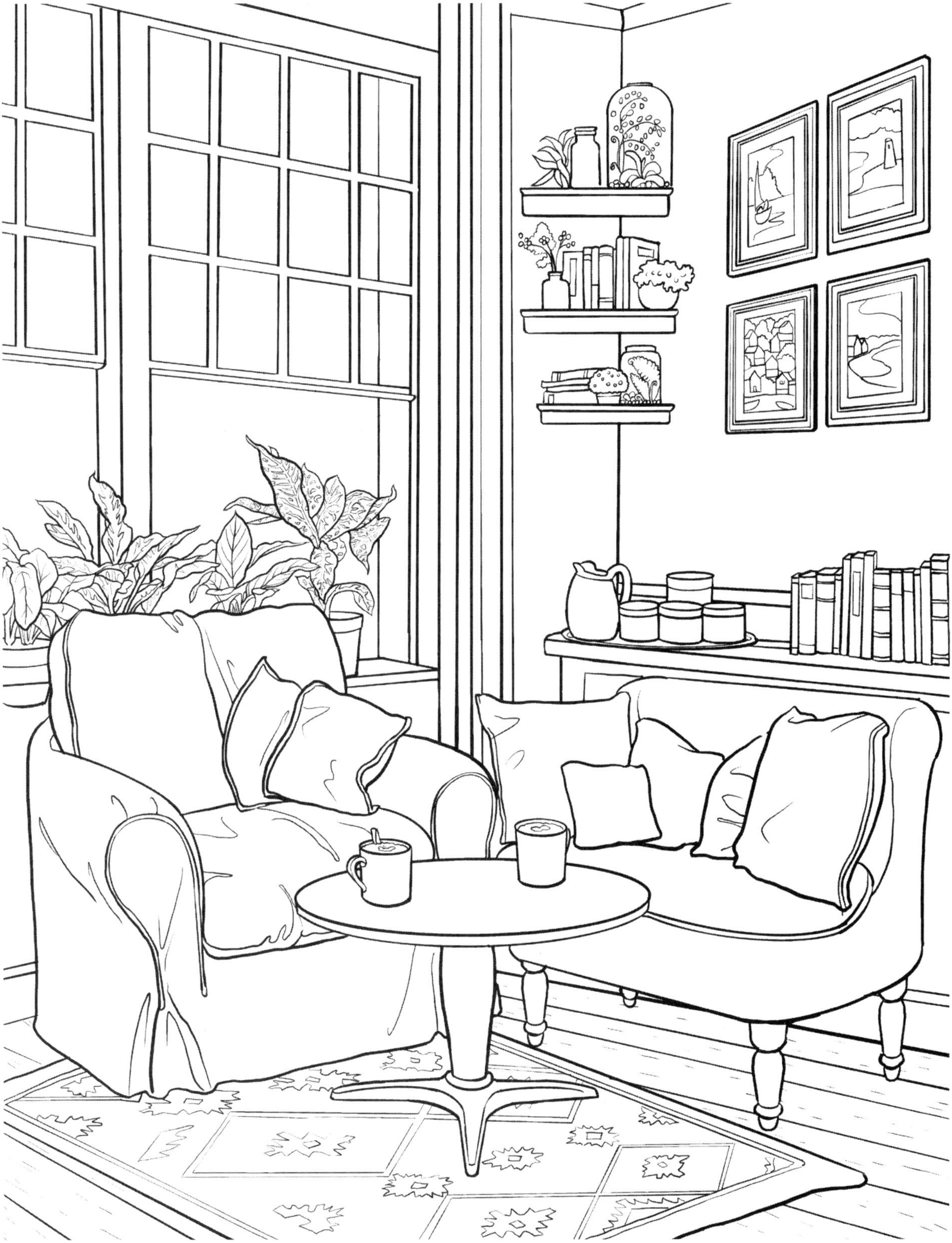

"Chunky scarves that looked like a grandmother had knitted them seemed to be integral to the look of Dream Harbor as well. And Jeanie didn't own a single pair of fingerless mittens. They should hand them out when you cross into town"

Cozy Season

"Farmers' market?
That's adorable"

Pumpkin Patch

"Logan leaned against the side of the truck, wiping the sweat from his brow. The sun was bright, and it was unseasonably warm today. There was a briny scent to the air, drifting in from the harbor"

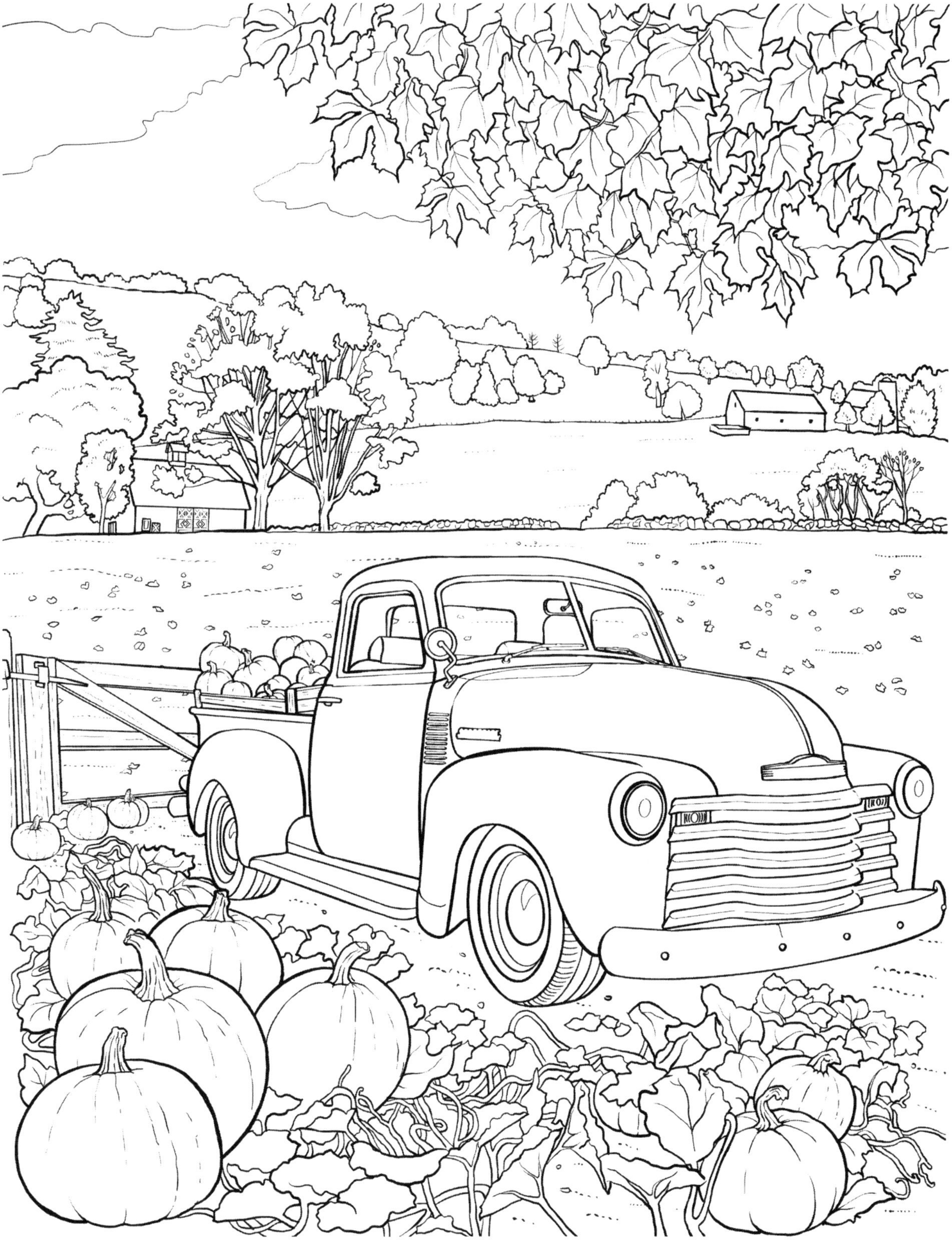

"She wanted to soak in all the autumnal excitement at the farm while it lasted"

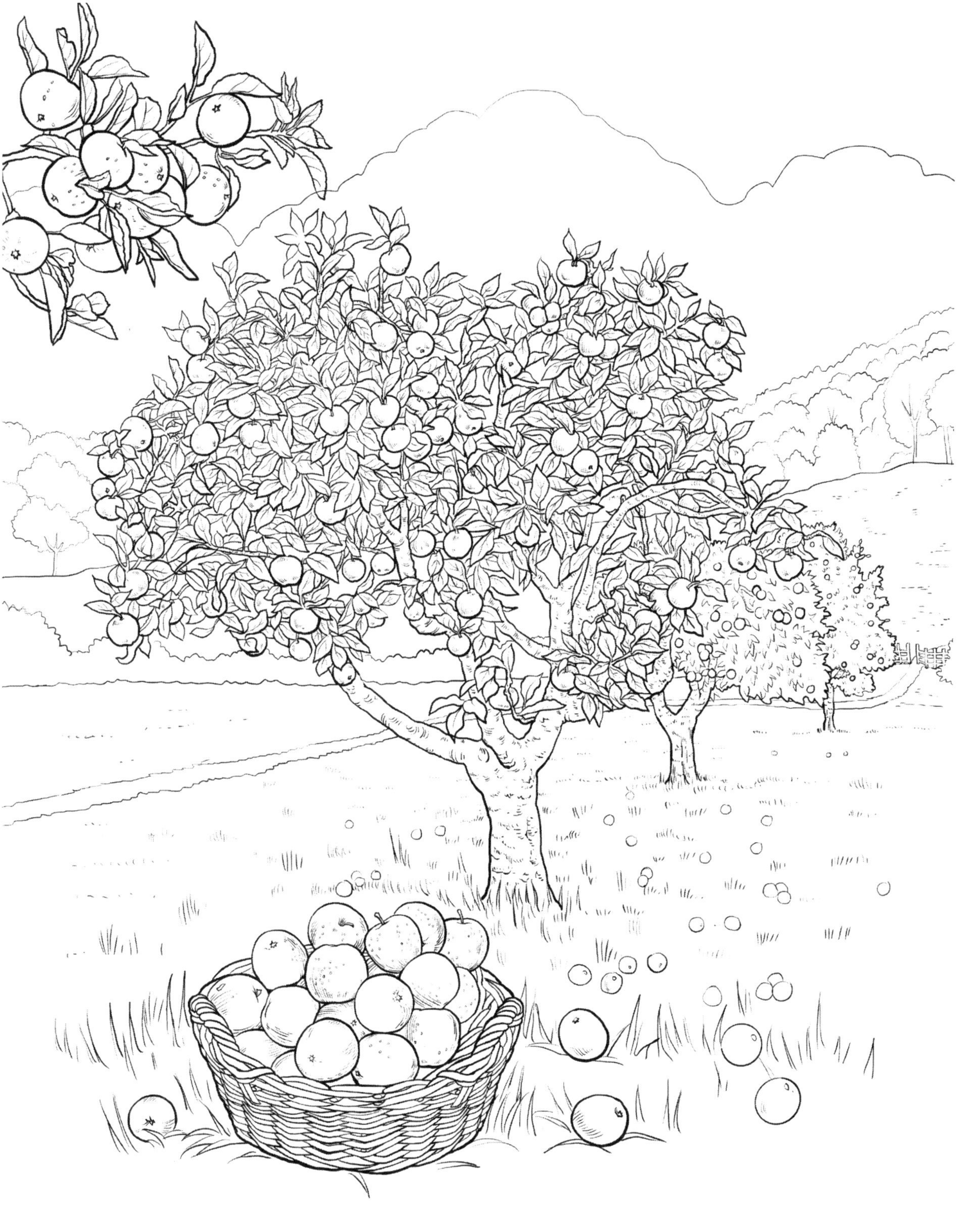

"But nearly halfway through October and the apples were almost done and even the pumpkin patch looked pretty picked over. The last big event of the season was the Fall Festival in town. Logan always supplied the pumpkins for the carving contest"

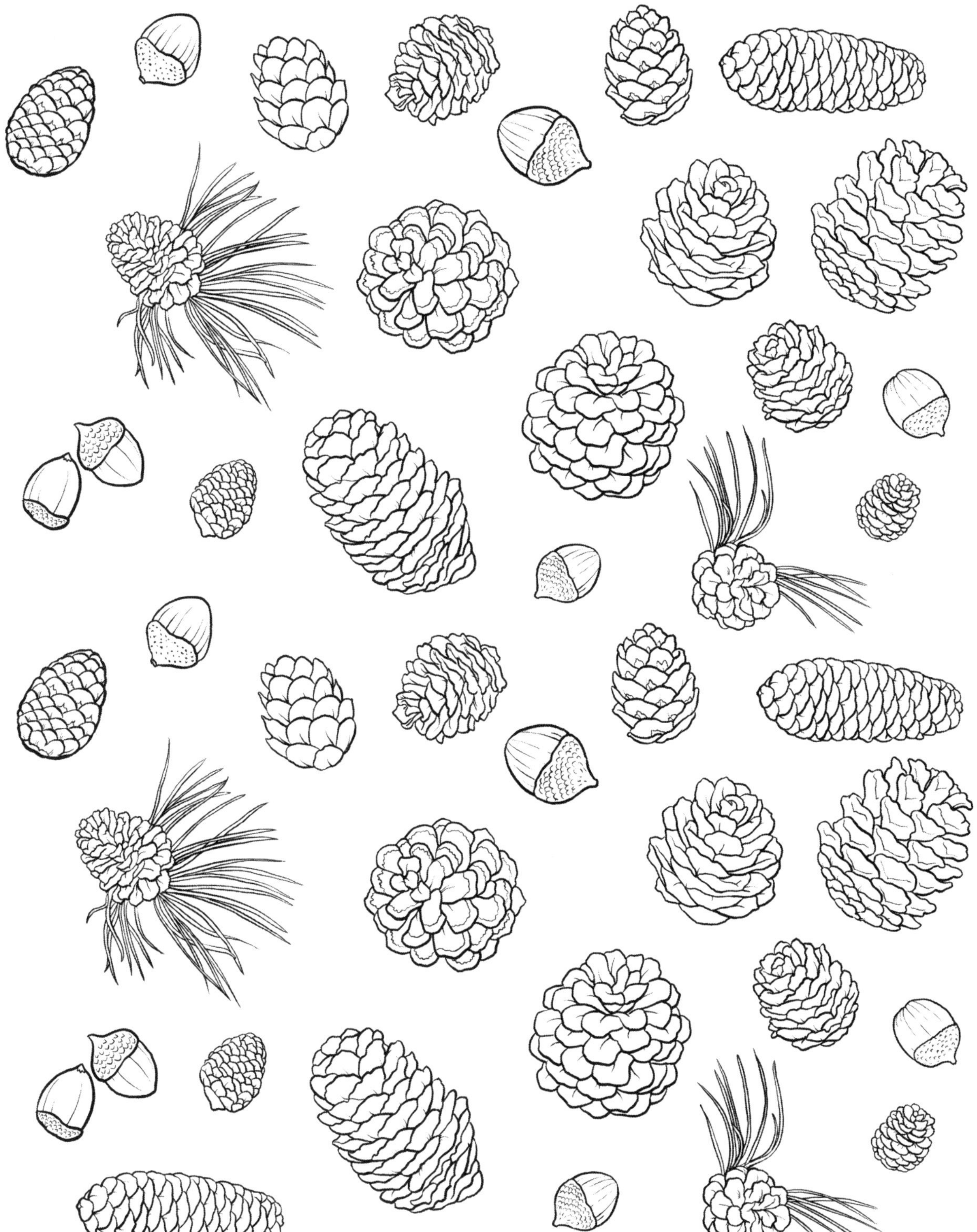

"He loved how early it got dark, how high and hot the bonfire grew, how the whole night felt cozy and spooky at once"

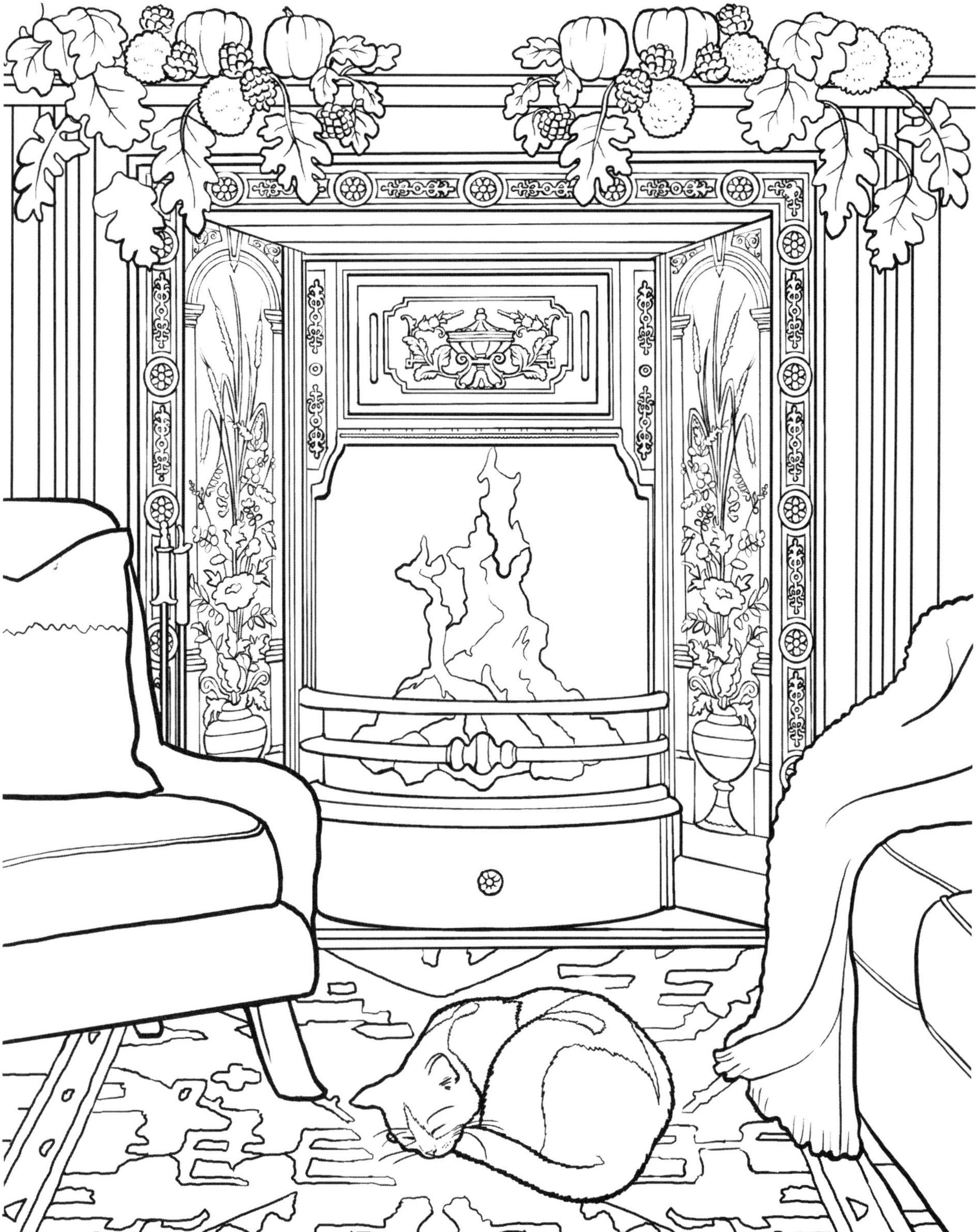

"True New Englanders love three things: the Red Sox, Dunkin's, and fall. Jeanie knew this, of course. She'd been one for the past decade, after all. But Dream Harbor's Fall Festival was a whole new level of autumnal worship"

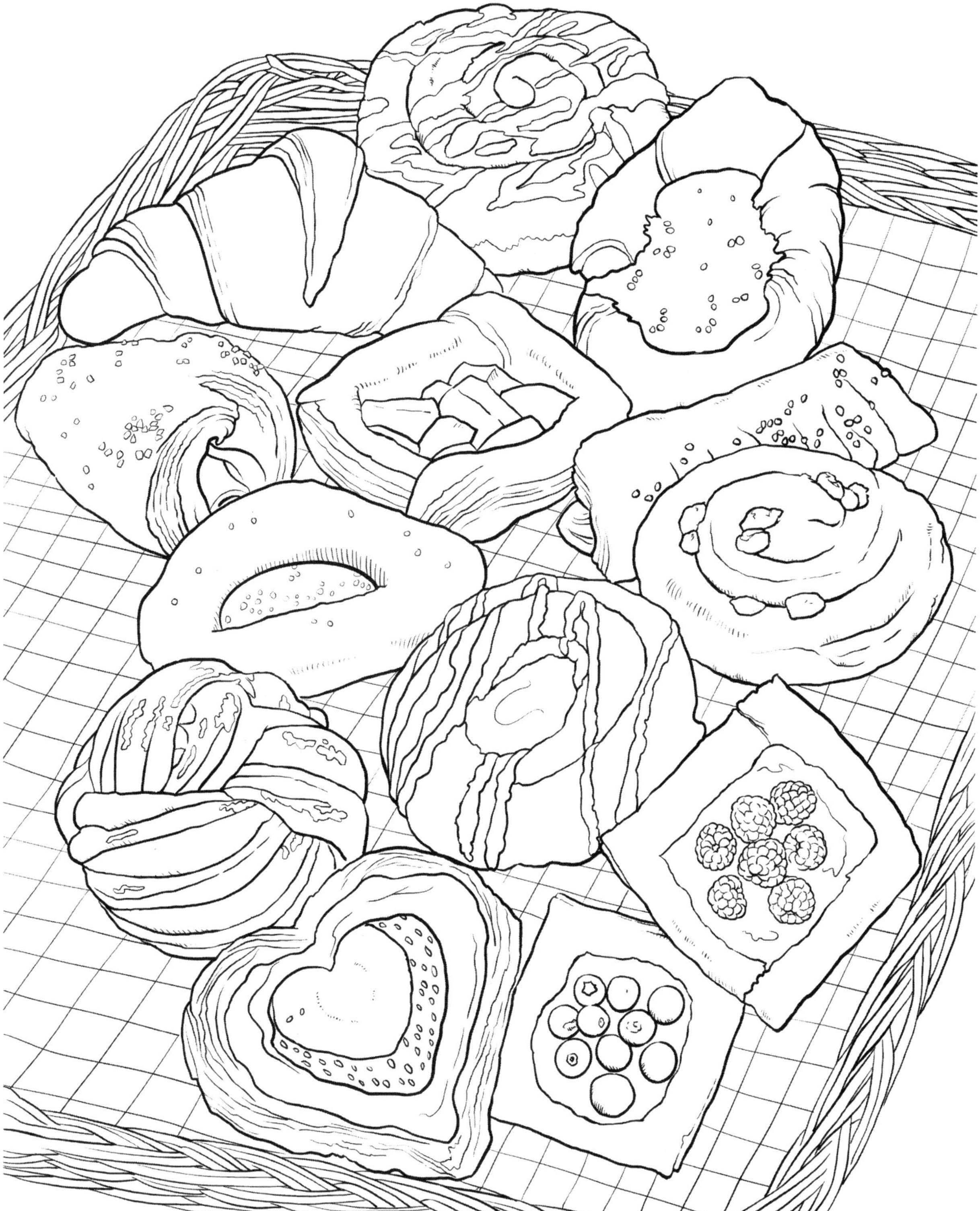

"See you tomorrow, bright and early, for my pumpkin-spiced latte!"

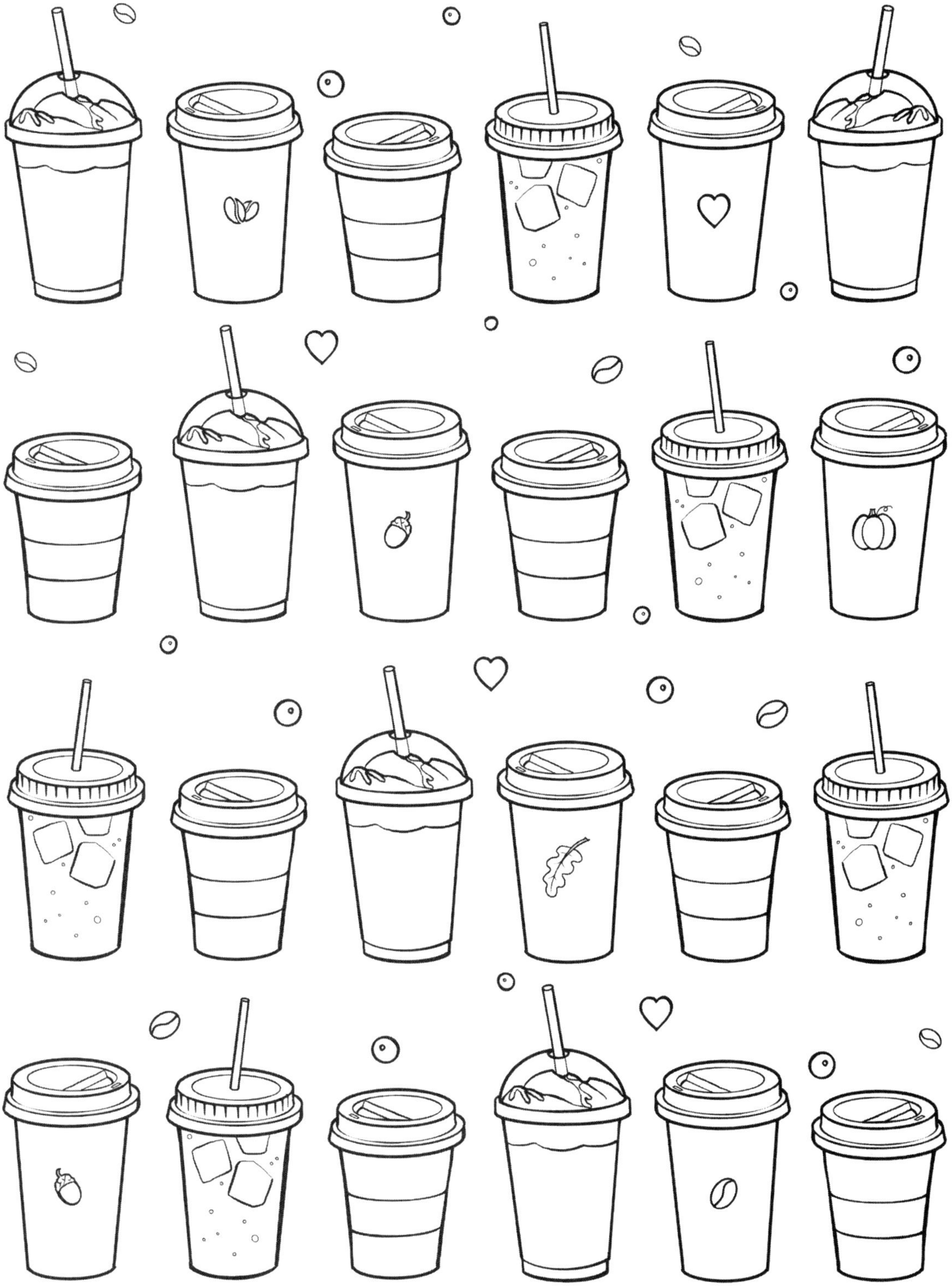

"Jeanie breathed in the warm hay and dry-leaf smell of the farm. A hint of woodsmoke and over-ripe apples drifted through the air"

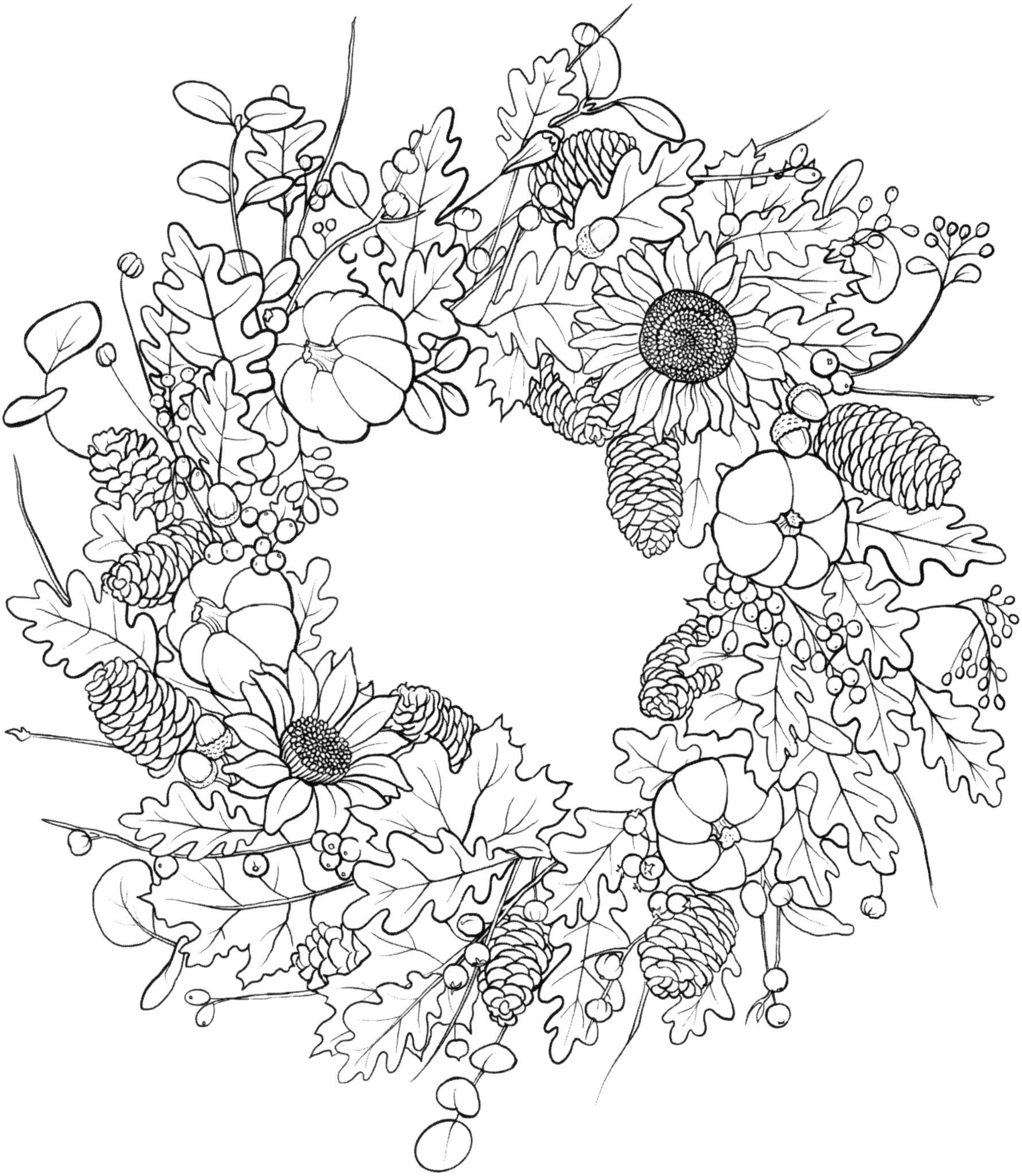

"The bakery case was lined with scones, muffins, and pumpkin-shaped sugar cookies for the morning"

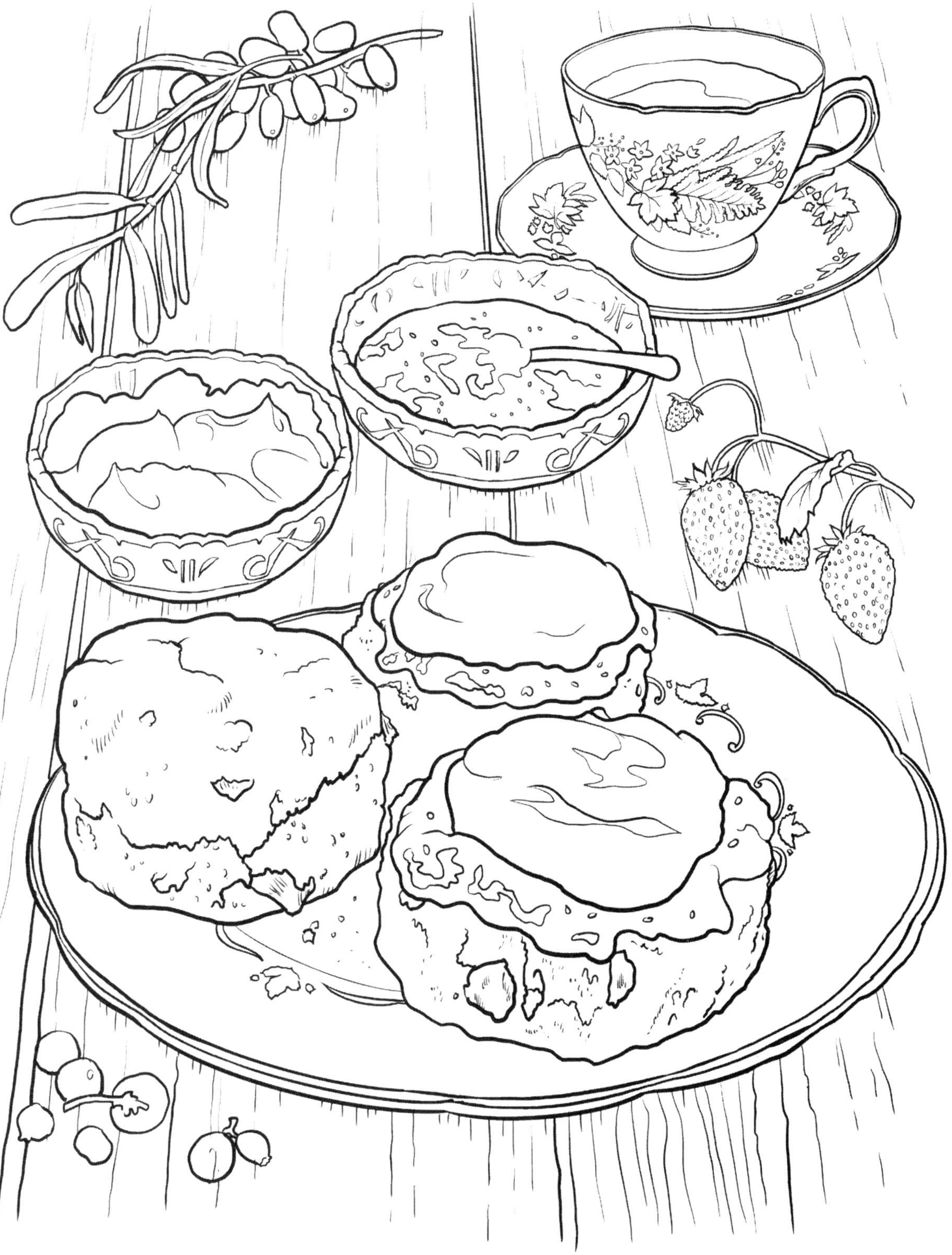

"The tiny surface was covered in empty mugs and well-loved paperbacks"

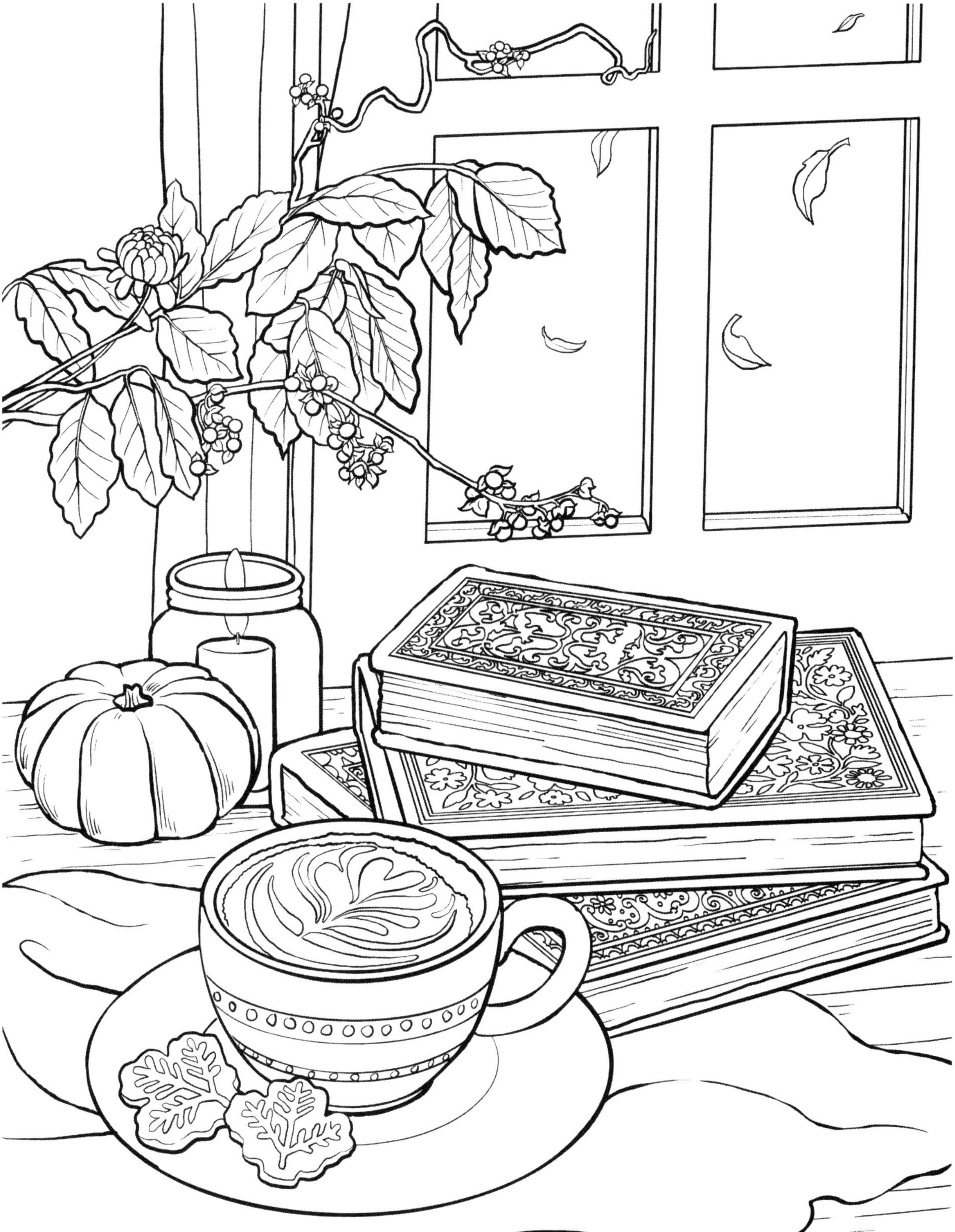

"The town square and surrounding streets were closed to traffic to accommodate the multitude of tents and tables and activities. There was pumpkin decorating, caramel apples, and cider donuts"

"The street itself was quaint and tidy, with trees lining the road. The leaves were just starting to change, mixing yellow and reds in with the green"

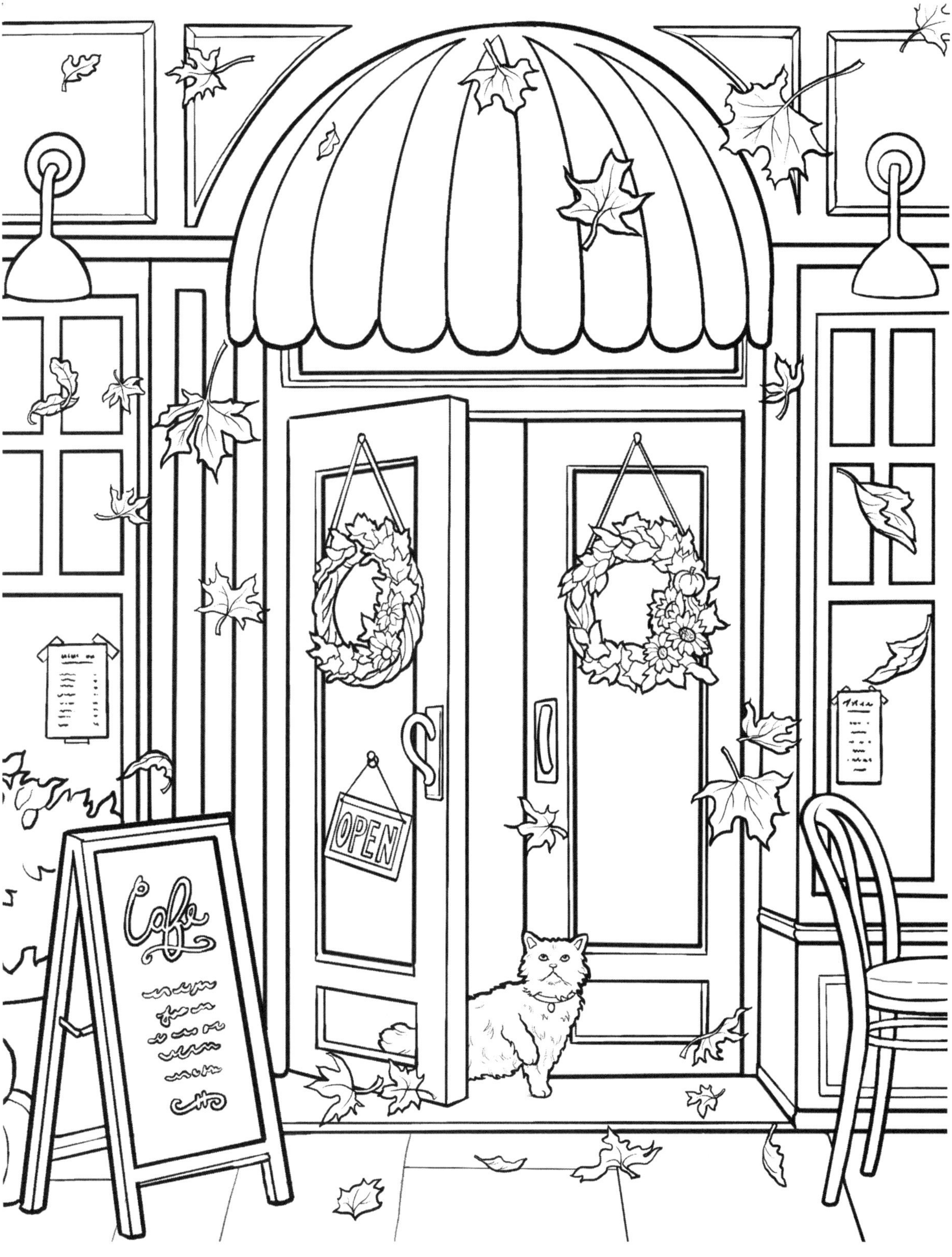
OPEN
Cafe

One More Chapter
a division of HarperCollinsPublishers Ltd
1 London Bridge Street
London SE1 9GF
www.harpercollins.co.uk
HarperCollinsPublishers
Macken House, 39/40 Mayor Street Upper,
Dublin 1, D01 C9W8, Ireland

First published by HarperCollinsPublishers Ltd 2025
This paperback edition published in 2025
Quotes from *The Pumpkin Spice Café*, 2023
2
Text Copyright © Laurie Gilmore 2023
Cover illustration © Kelley McMorris
Internal illustrations by Nicolette Cavern

A catalogue record for this book is available from the British Library
ISBN: 978-0-00-875985-8

Printed and bound in the United States

All rights reserved. No part of this publication may be reproduced, stored in a retrieval system, or transmitted, in any form or by any means, electronic, mechanical, photocopying, recording or otherwise, without the prior permission of the publishers.

Without limiting the author's and publisher's exclusive rights, any unauthorised use of this publication to train generative artificial intelligence (AI) technologies is expressly prohibited. HarperCollins also exercise their rights under Article 4(3) of the Digital Single Market Directive 2019/790 and expressly reserve this publication from the text and data mining exception.

The DREAM HARBOR SERIES

Sign up to Laurie's newsletter or follow her at: thelauriegilmore.com

Maddy
Learns From Her
GARDEN

ISBN 978-1-0980-5791-6 (paperback)
ISBN 978-1-0980-2992-0 (hardcover)
ISBN 978-1-0980-2993-7 (digital)

Copyright © 2021 by Timothy Wright

All rights reserved. No part of this publication may be reproduced, distributed, or transmitted in any form or by any means, including photocopying, recording, or other electronic or mechanical methods without the prior written permission of the publisher. For permission requests, solicit the publisher via the address below.

Christian Faith Publishing, Inc.
832 Park Avenue
Meadville, PA 16335
www.christianfaithpublishing.com

Printed in the United States of America

Maddy
Learns From Her
GARDEN

Timothy Wright

1

When I'm in my garden, I'm learning all the time, and questions of heaven keep going through my mind.

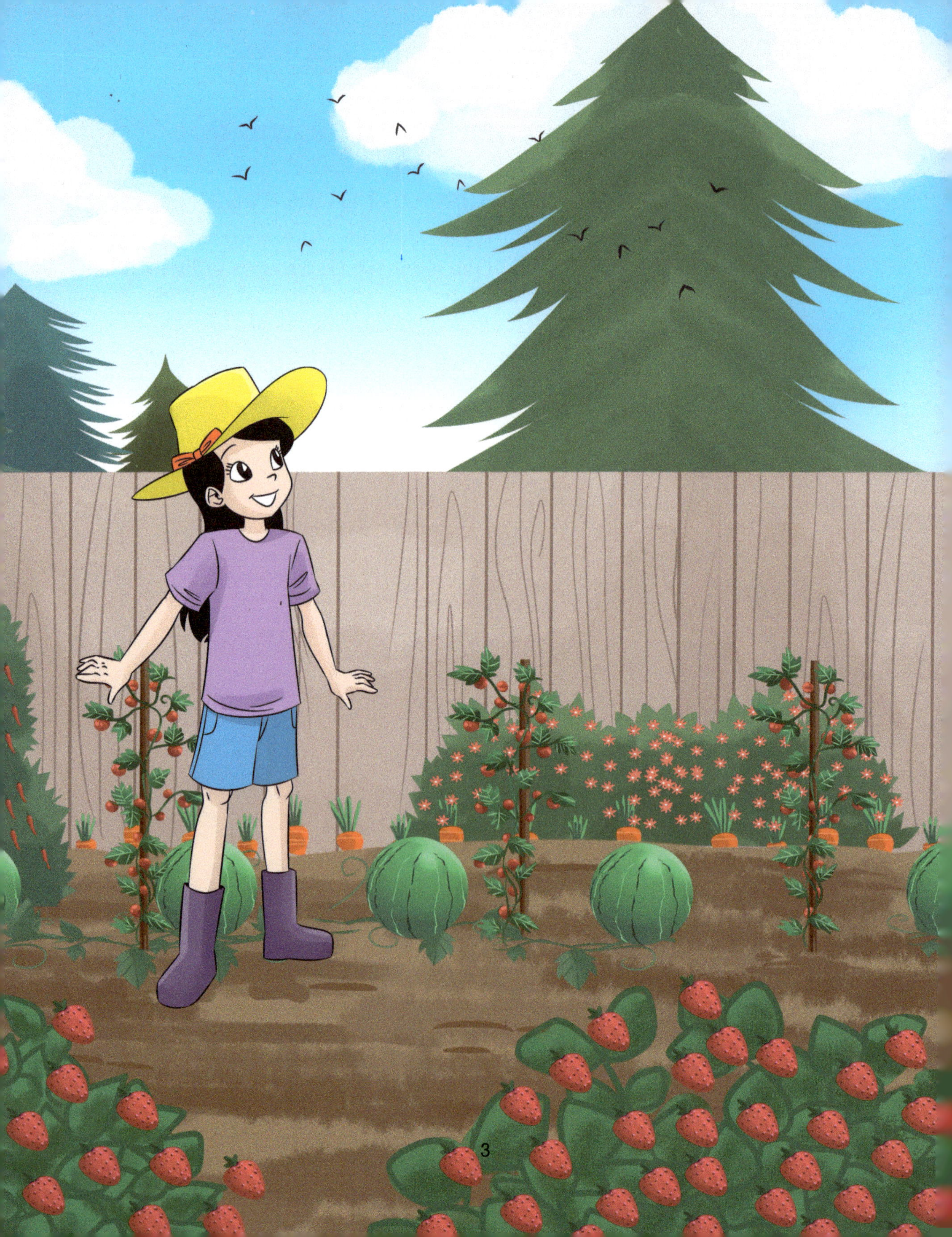

How do I get there because I can't fly? Mommy tells me that angels bring me there when I die.

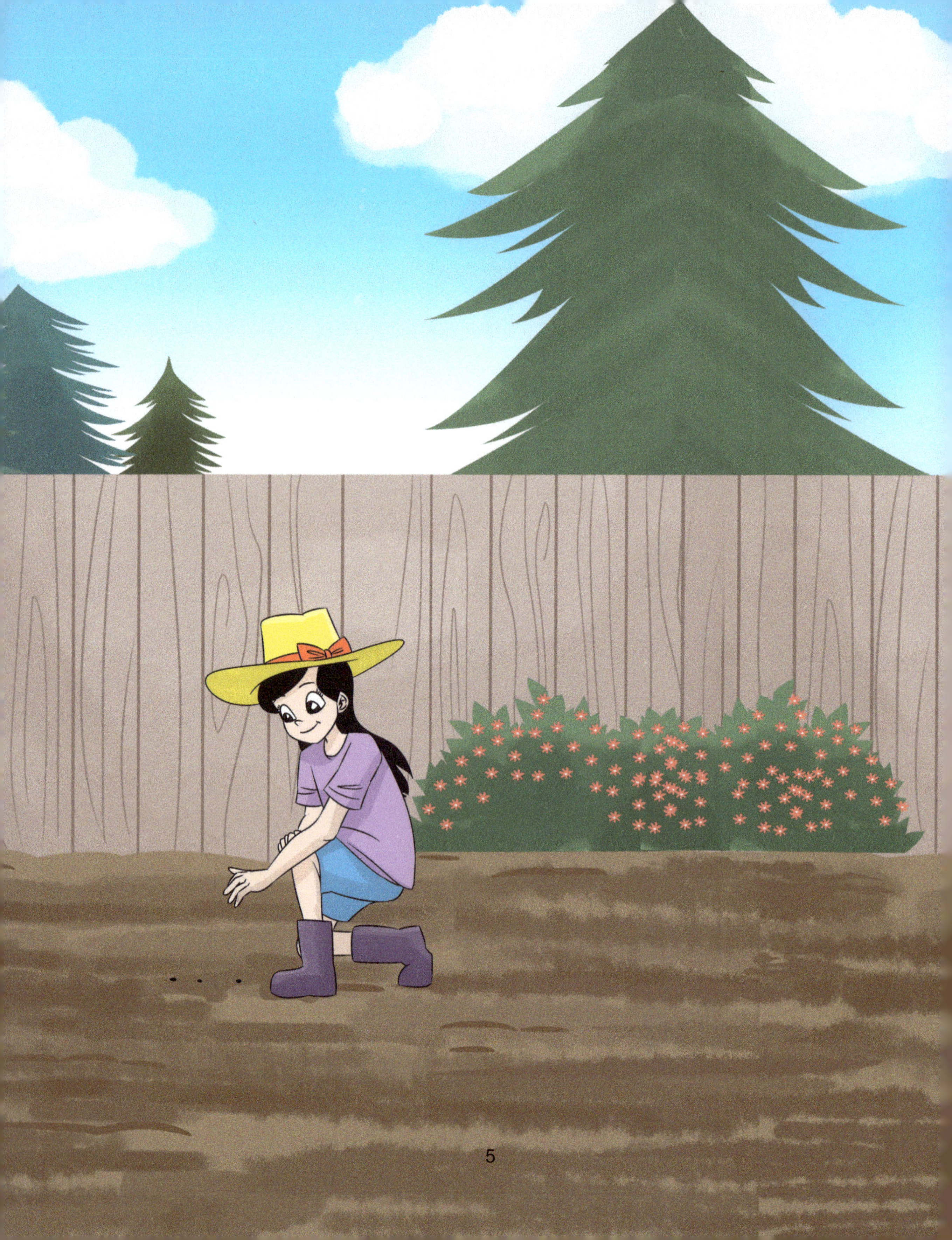

Did you know that a garden can help you understand that even when you die, you can still live again?

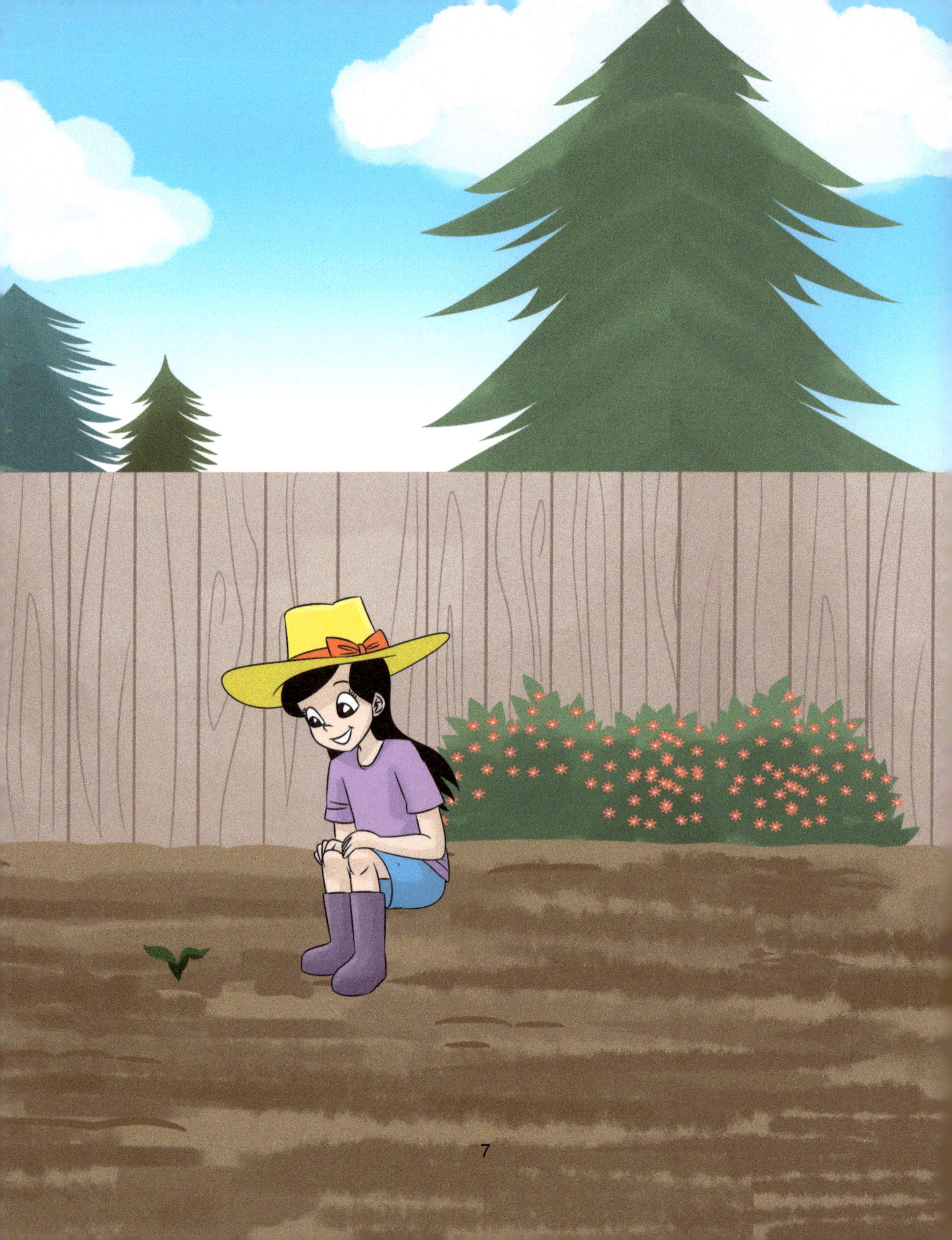

When you plant a seed before it will show, it first has to die, then the plant starts to grow.

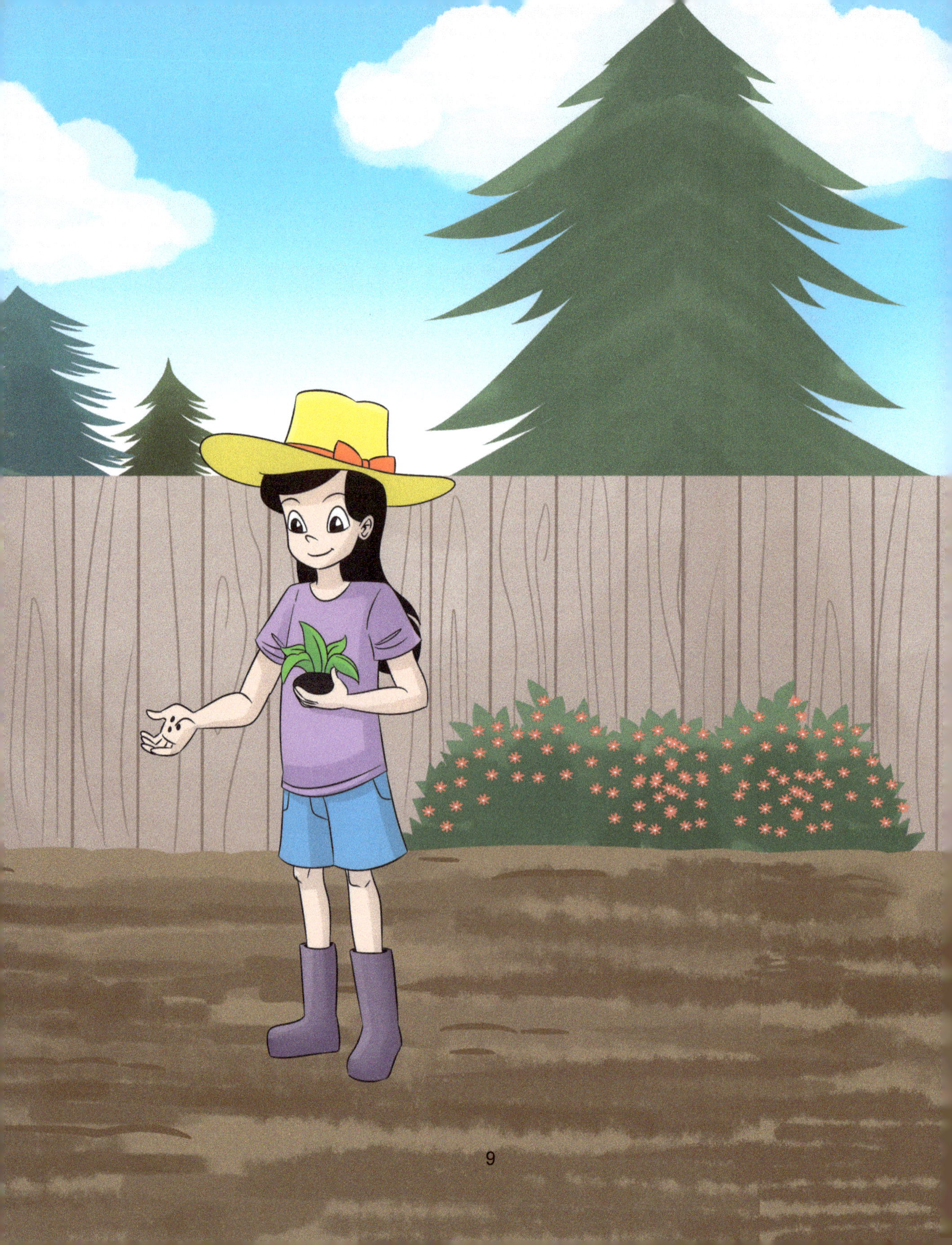

When I get to heaven, I'm still going to be me...but the seed that God planted will look different, you see.

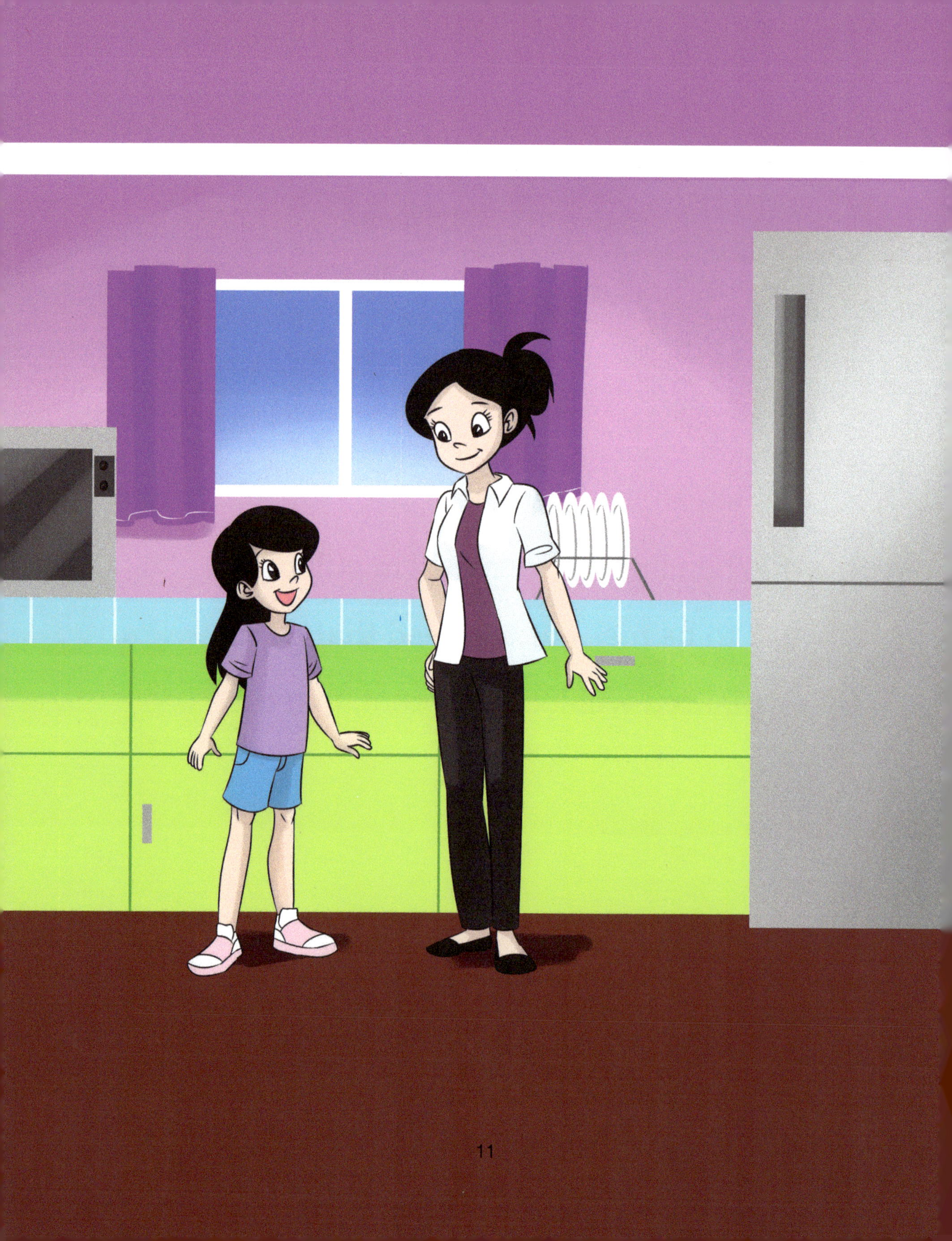

Mommy tells me the questions that go through my head, God has all the answers in my Bible, she said.

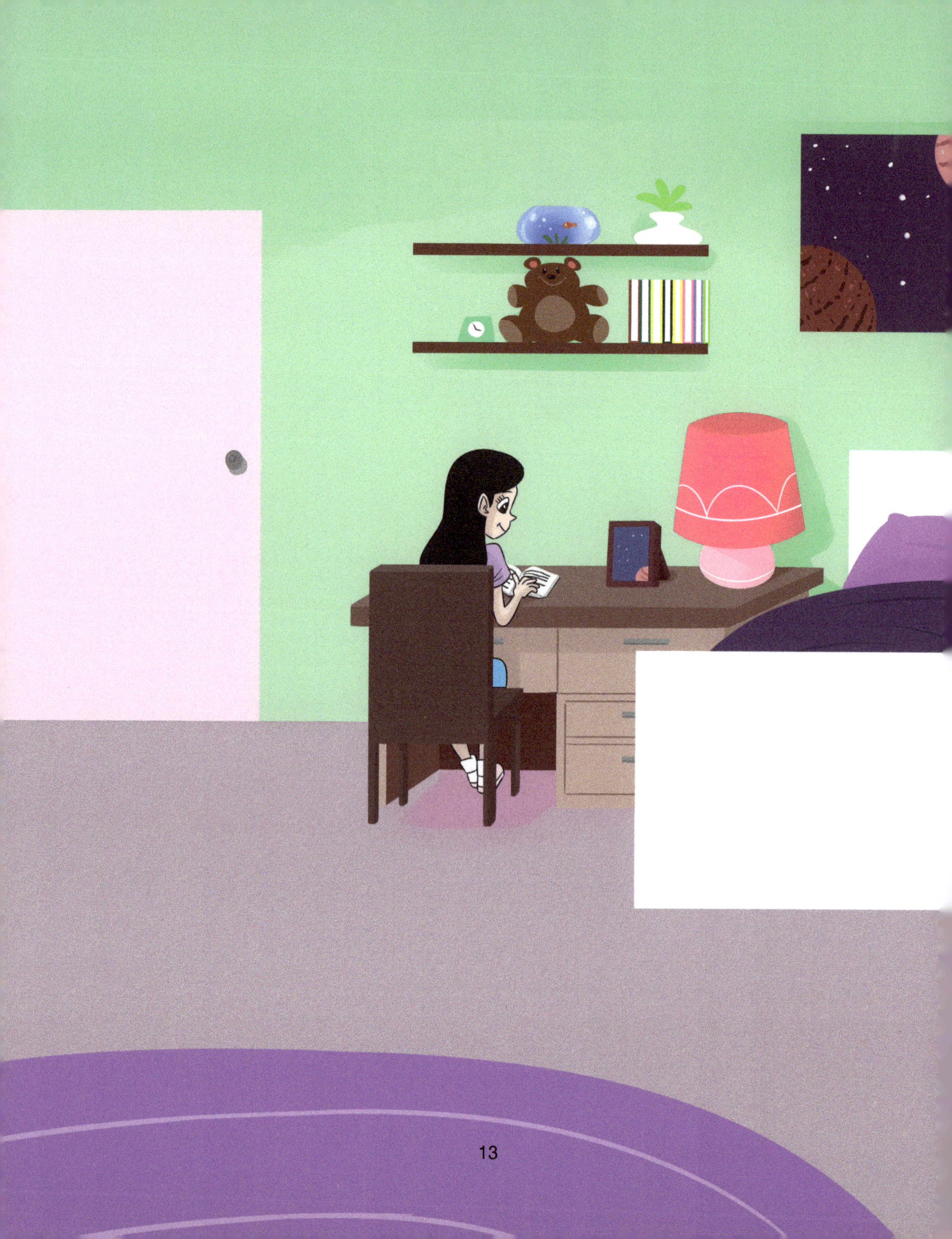

So when I read my Bible, I'm beginning to see...It was God who put all these questions in me.

15

But what will I wear when I'm in heaven with Him? These questions keep coming again and again.

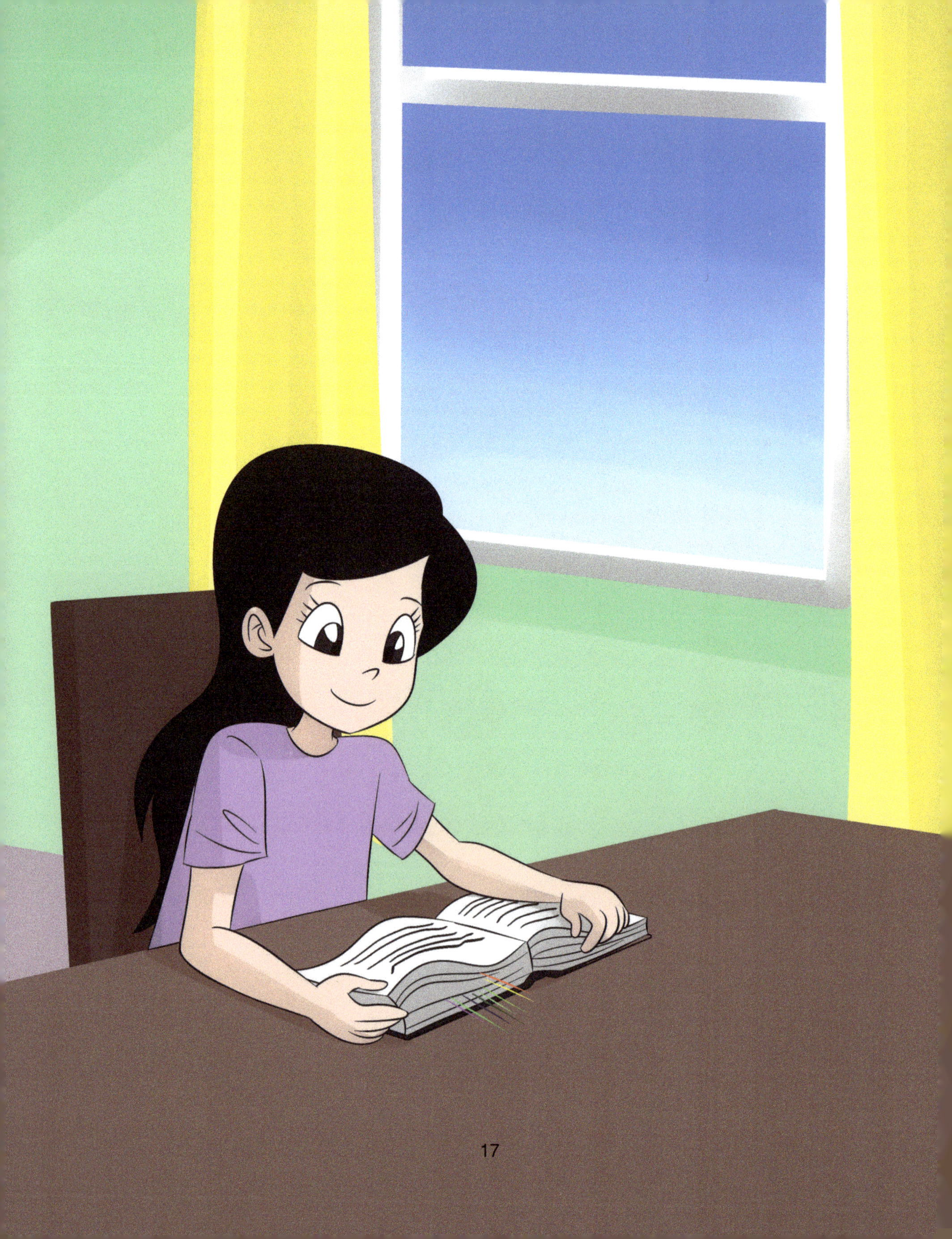

I'll put off the old and put on the new...my Bible says in heaven, that's what I'll do.

19

I'm still not too sure how I get from here to there...then Mommy said something that made it so clear.

21

When I fall asleep, and I'm not in
my bed, but in the morning, I am...
that's like heaven, she said.

So we fall asleep here and wake
up there...now that makes it
simple, so easy, and clear.

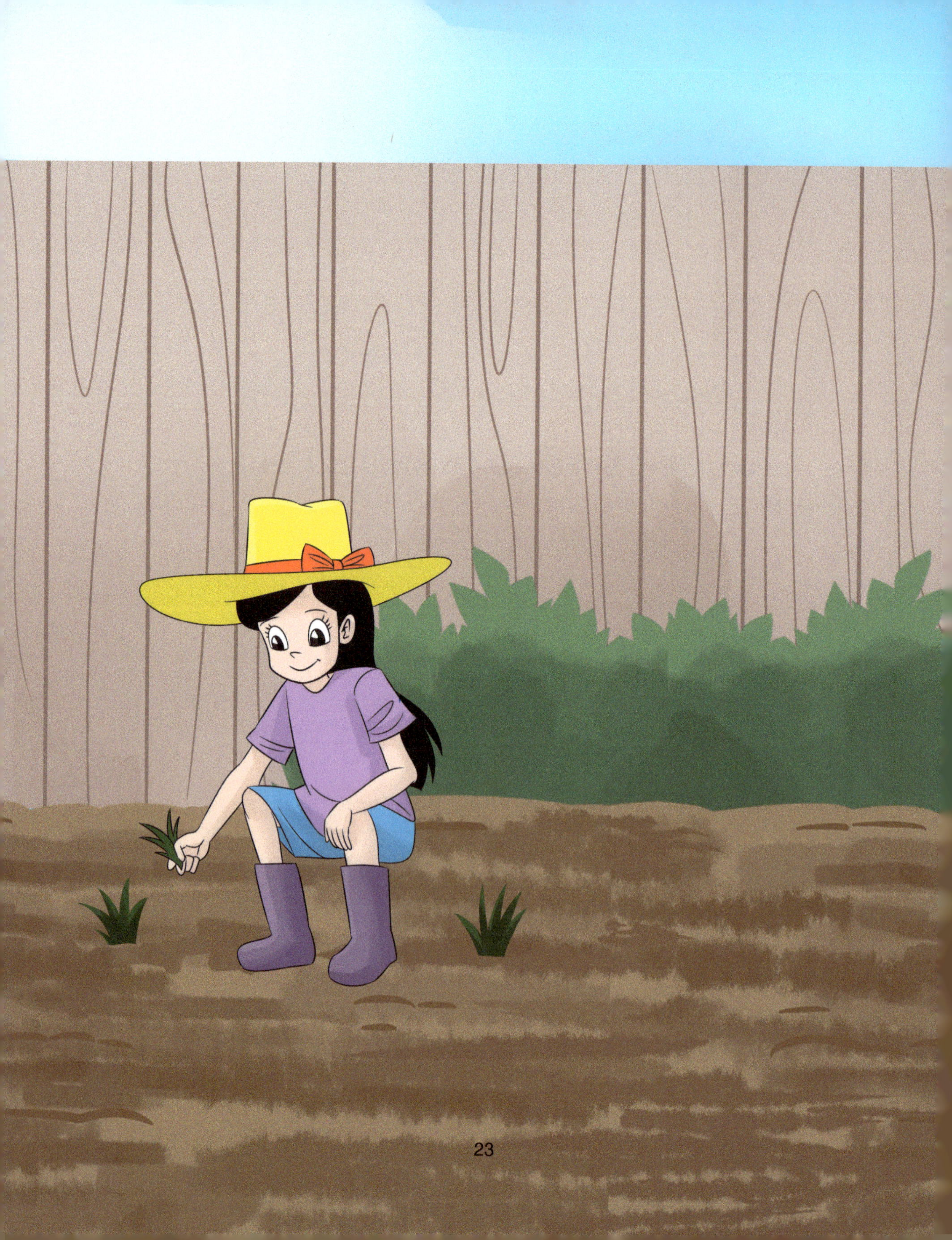

God teaches me things in my garden each day as I'm pulling out weeds that get in my way.

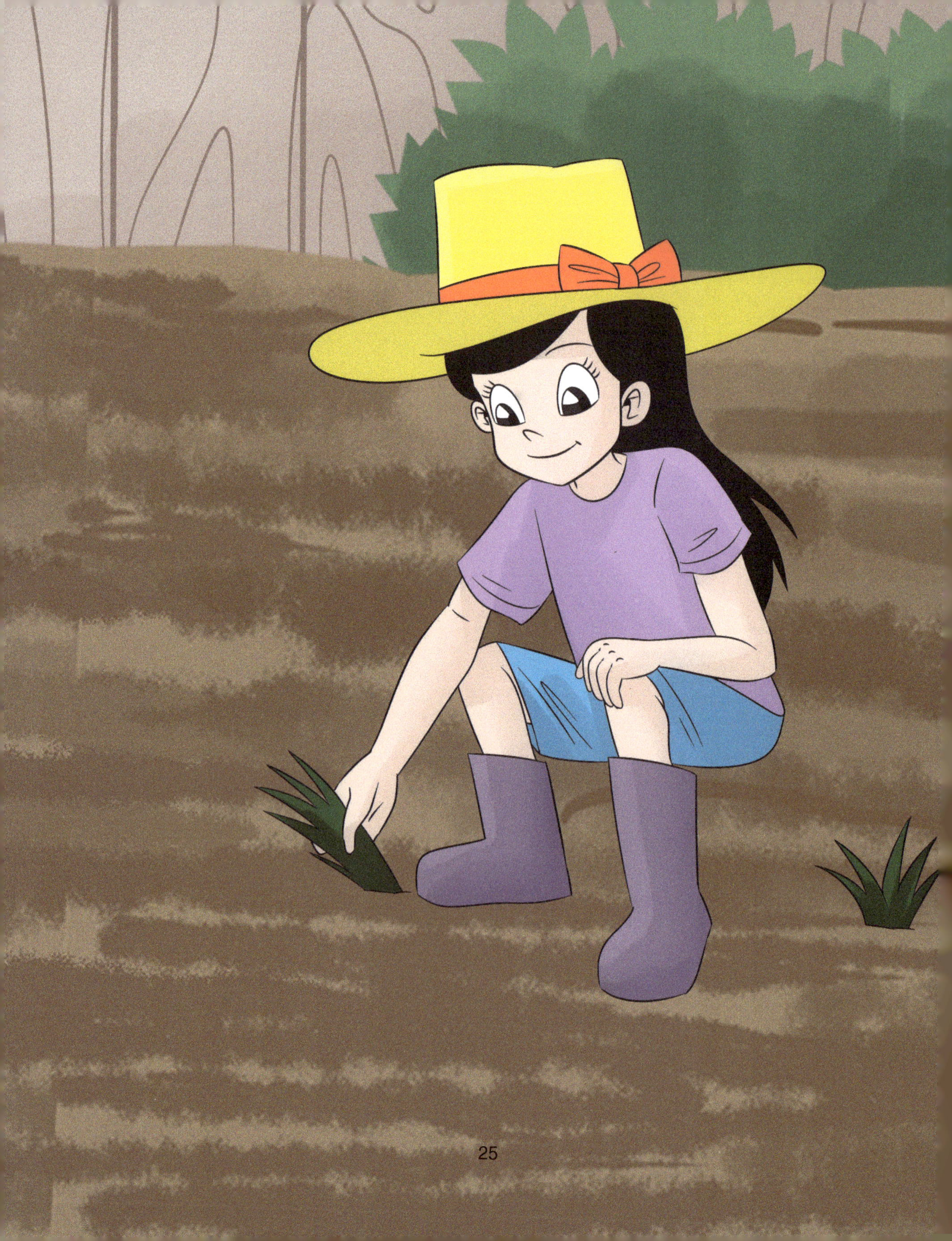

Sometimes I'm angry, and sometimes I'm mad...these are like weeds that make my heart sad.

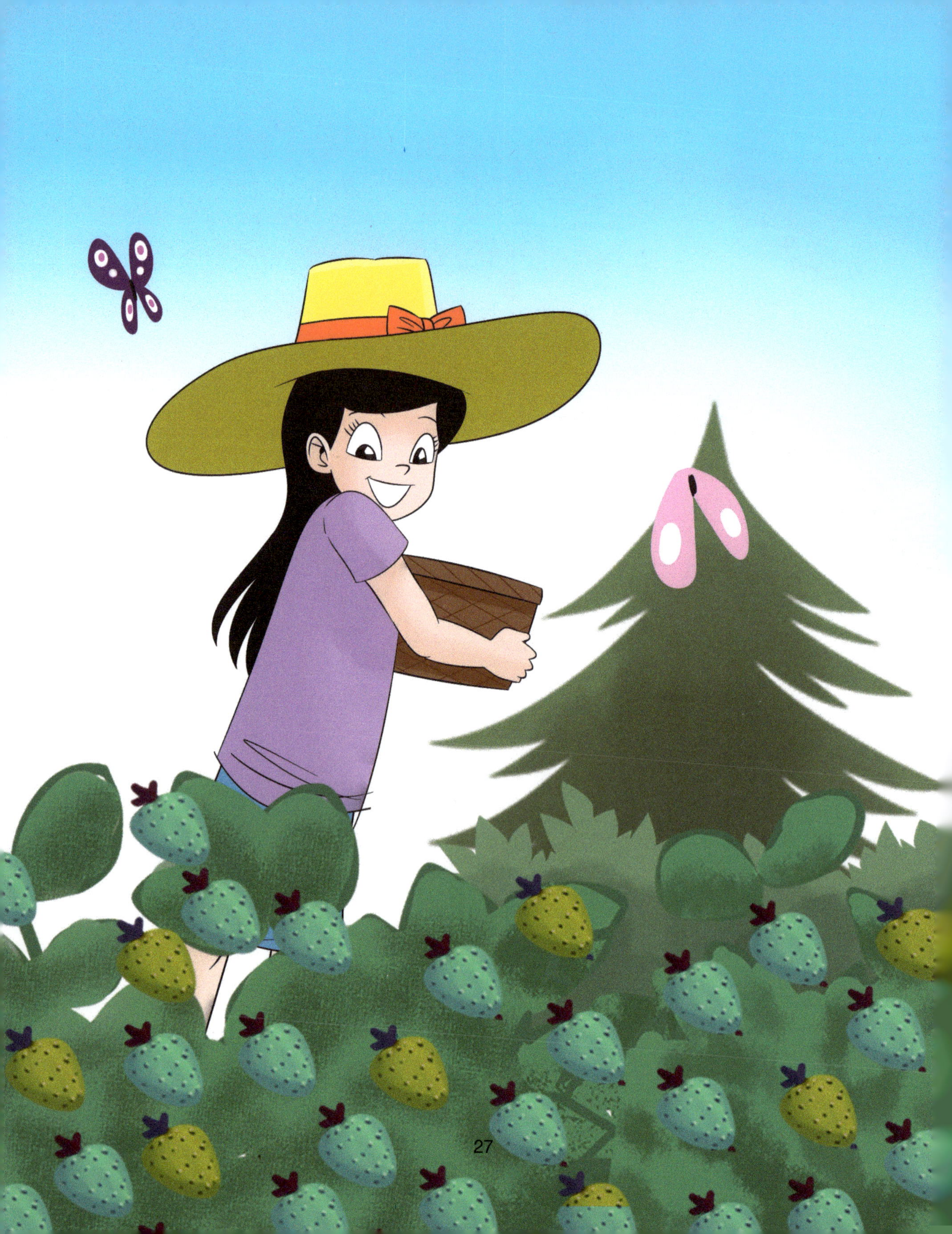

My garden teaches me to be patient and wait. If I pick things too soon, they don't taste so great.

29

When I'm faithful to Jesus, His seed starts to grow. When I give Him my heart, His fruit starts to show.

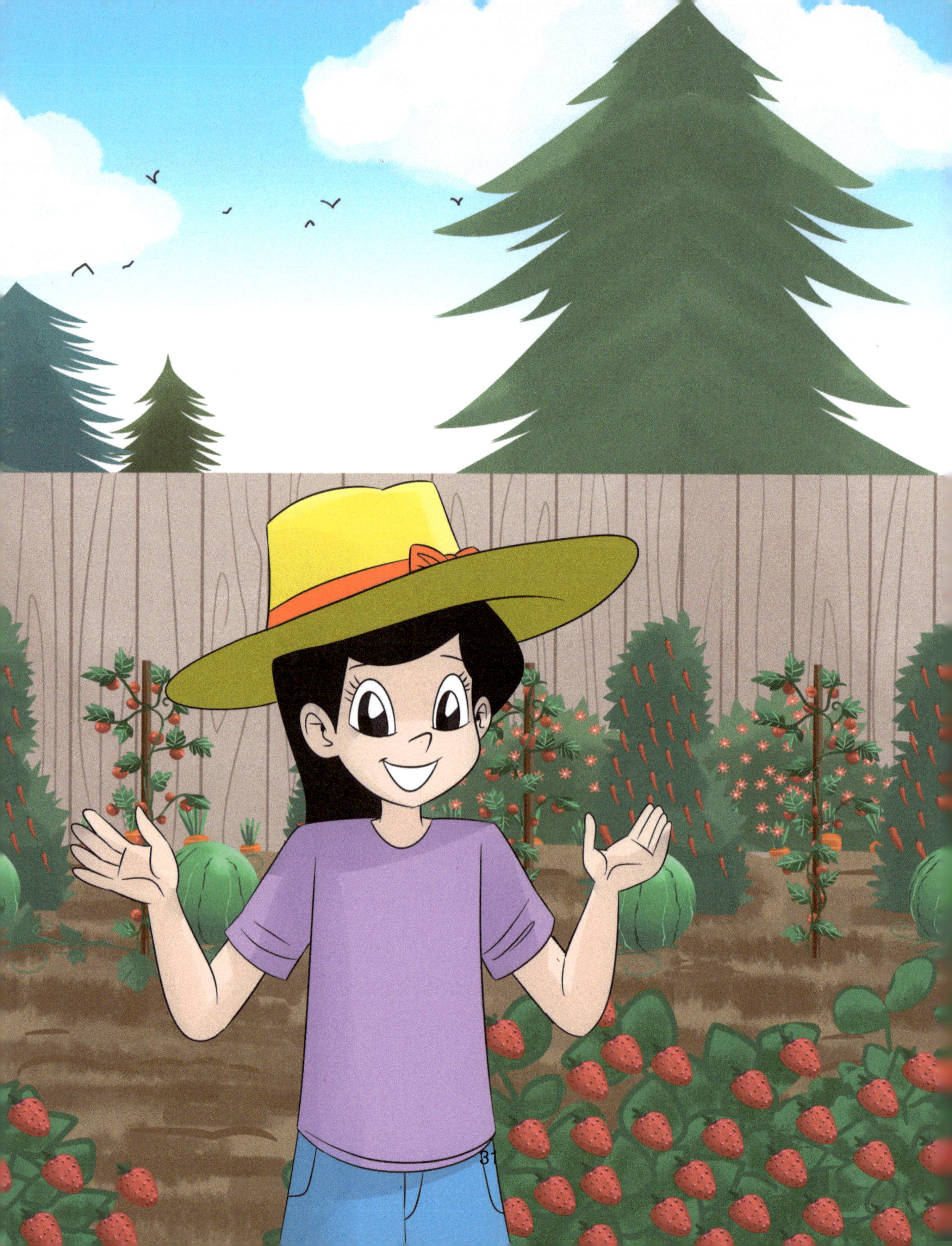

Do you see how a garden can teach us about Him? So don't be discouraged when you put your seeds in.

33

Tomatoes get ripe when they stay on the vine, but there's one thing they need...they need lots of time.

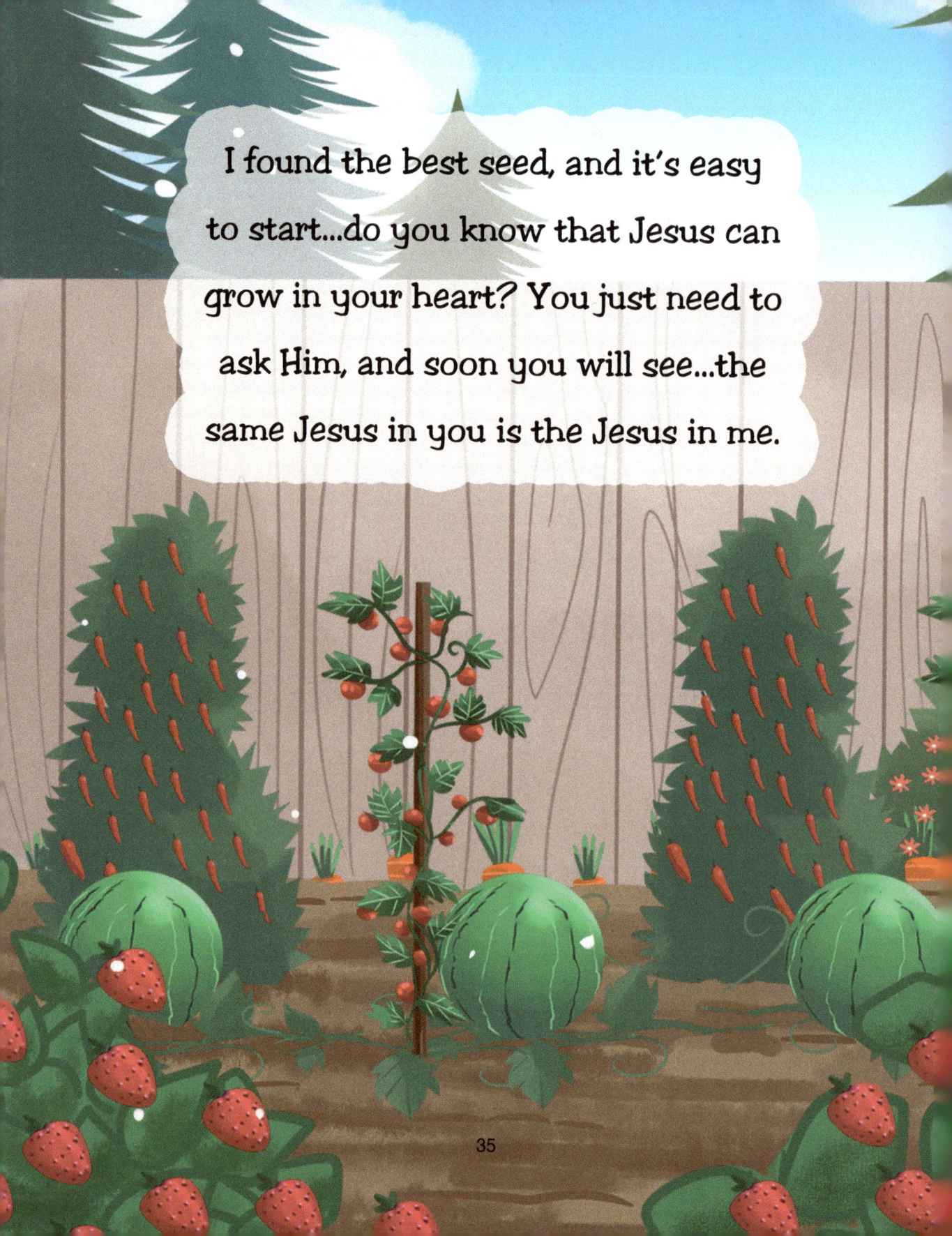

I found the best seed, and it's easy to start...do you know that Jesus can grow in your heart? You just need to ask Him, and soon you will see...the same Jesus in you is the Jesus in me.

Hey, the sun's going down, and I must go too, but it sure has been fun talking to you.

37

So don't forget to take time for Jesus today.

Remember, He's always just a prayer away.

About the Author

Timothy Wright had fun writing about Maddy and what God was teaching her in her garden. In all reality, it has been what God has taught him because he also loves to garden. He and his wife have nineteen grandchildren, and it is their desire to see all of them come to a saving knowledge of Jesus. He doesn't know how long he can keep writing, but as Moses prayed to God to help him number his days, so he prays. He has been writing over forty years but only this last year has pursued publishing a book. This will be his eighth book, and he hopes to write many more for God's glory.

CPSIA information can be obtained
at www.ICGtesting.com
Printed in the USA
LVHW071301030921
696885LV00002B/10